TALES
from
OLD CAROLINA

By F. ROY JOHNSON

Traditional and Historical Sketches

Of the Area Between and About
the Chowan River and Great Dismal Swamps

Published by
JOHNSON PUBLISHING COMPANY
Murfreesboro, North Carolina

Copyright 1965
Library of Congress Card No. 65-8878
1980 Reprint of 1965 and 1967
ISBN 0-930230-38-8

Contents

Illustrations

Legends, Myths and Stories

vi

PART 1

The North Carolina Myth

CHAPTER I

"Half you hear at home (in Alabama) about North Carolinians having rings about their legs from picking whortle berries in the flat ponds, and having no hair on their breasts from frequently climbing persimmon trees is 'all bosh.' "

Thus during the Civil War an Alabamian sets about to explode the old and widely circulated myth that North Carolina was a backward and primitive state peopled by ignorant, poor and lawless characters.

He was visiting Gates County with Benning's Brigade, Hood's Division, and wrote a letter dated April 27, 1863, to the "Montgomery (Alabama) Mail."

Encamped five miles from Gatesville, county seat of Gates County, he liked what he saw of the prosperous plantation country, one of the earliest settled in North Carolina. Locked between the Chowan River and the Dismal Swamp next to the Virginia border, isolation had made it a quaint cultural island where colonial manners and customs of the English and Scotch settlers—and the nature wisdom of the Indian—were preserved.

Here was a set of laborous and independent agriculturalists "primitive in their habits—hospitable to an exceeding degree who bid the stranger welcome to their fireside and table without price or money."

The greening plains between the great mysterious

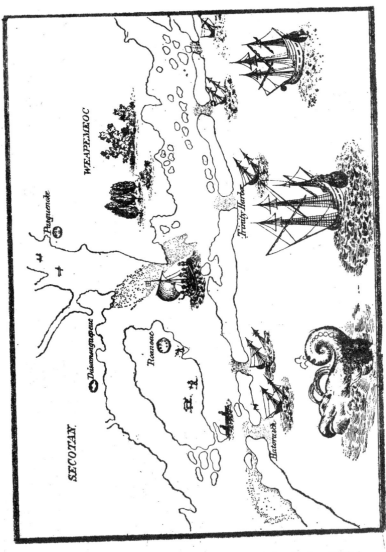

Arrival of the Englishmen in Virginia 1584
from de Bry

swamps was strictly rural with the winter wheat "springing forth in the most beautiful proportions on every side of the splendid roads we traverse." Corn, the chief grain, was ready for planting and field hands ant-like activated the plantations on each hand.

The quaint countryside reflected none of the influence exerted by the villages and towns in some of the neighboring counties.

Here, elegant mansions were spaced about at equal intervals with the plantations, and between these numbers of poor people lived in one-room houses. Grain being the chief product of the farms, barns ten times the size of the residence and the two-wheel cart were commonly seen.

The ladies were neatly dressed, well behaved, and had "none of those 'highfalutin' airs so common among the mushroom aristocracy further down south." They took pride in their skill at cooking, washing, spinning and weaving.

Three Distinctly Different Areas

While customs were strikingly colonial-like, lore had developed more than ordinary variety. Perhaps this was because the country was divided into three distinctly different areas, with all having unique physical and social backgrounds.

West of the central plantations lay the sand barrens, an area which looked much like the North Carolina Sand Hills, and beyond them the deep Chowan River pocosins. These pocosins were overgrown with cypress and juniper trees, and spaced about the swamps were the sandy ridges covered with large pines. This was the famed tar and turpentine country with its fabled poor, clannish and fighting inhabitants—where for more than a century customs had successfully resisted change.

Here fabled "Scratch Hall" happily clung to simple

[3]

ways and independent and unrestrained manners of its pioneer forbears. So contented were its people they would stir themselves to make few changes during the next half of a century.

Scratch Hall and its natives had been fabilized much like North Carolina during its turbulent beginning. Even a century after the Civil War still current was the fable that a Scratch Hall girl's age could be determined by counting the scum rings she had collected while berry picking in the flat ponds. Likewise, the Scratch Hall man had no hair on his breast from scurrying up and down persimmon trees.

Even though the story tellers of northeastern North Carolina and southeastern Virginia enjoyed Scratch Hall fables and fairy tales, the Hall people were greatly admired for their independence and individualism.

East of the central plantations stretched the Great Dismal Swamp which erected such an impenetrable barrier that it vexed the imagination of everyone—local people, neighbors and travelers.

From the swamp's mysterious depths came a great variety of lore—from the early colonial period to recent years. The swamp inspired legends about the Indian hunter and English explorer. In the early eighteenth century William Byrd found it a great unexplored "desart," and in the latter half, George Washington was intrigued by its natural resources. From the Revolution to the Civil War it served as a sanctuary for run-away slaves and other people who wished to escape civilization. Various generations of border settlers contributed stories about grotesque creatures, monsters, hermits, lost people, wild people, lost treasure, the devil, witches and fairies.

A collection of much of the lore and literature relating to this fabled country may be found in the several parts and chapters of this work.

Primeval Hunting Ground

CHAPTER II

Utilized by Numerous Indian Groups

Pre-historic artifacts, collected by archeologists during recent years, indicate that the area extending eastward from the Chowan River to the Great Dismal Swamp was utilized by numerous Indian groups over a period of several centuries.

John White's map is the first documentary prop to its usage. This map shows the areas both east and west of the Chowan River to be in possession of the "Chawanook" Indians, a name meaning "they of the south."

The map was based on findings of a 1586 expedition by the English from Fort Raleigh who raised their sails to the wind and ascended the gentle waters of the Chowan River to learn first hand about King Menatonon and his kingdom of "Chawanook" which professed friendship and boasted of 700 fighting men.

Of this expedition Ralph Lane wrote to Sir Walter Raleigh,

"Between Muscamunge and Chawanook upon the left hand, is a goodly high land, and there is a town which we call The Blind Town, but the savages call it Ohanoak, and it has a very good corn field belonging unto it. It is subject to Chawanook."

Indian Fairy Tales

Of the right, the east side of the river which embraced almost a hundred miles to the Atlantic coast, Lane made no mention. He was concerned chiefly with the temper of the natives, their fighting strength, location of fabled "Chaunis Temoatin," city of the Mangoacs, where the savages "beautify their houses with great plates" of a soft, pale yellow metal thought to be gold, and pearls produced in deep waters of the northeast.

The Indian fairy tales, represented as the truth, fascinated the English. Both Menatonon and the savages of Moratoc, who lived upon the river by that name, told of "strange things" thirty or forty days journey westward "at the head of the river."

The source of the mysterious stream of Moratoc (later the Roanoke), they said, "springs out of a main rock, in that abundance, that forthwith makes a most violent stream; and further, that this huge rock stands so near unto the sea, that many times in storms (the wind coming outwardly from the sea) the waves thereof are beaten into the said fresh stream, so that the fresh water for a certain space, grows salty and brackish."

Country of the Wild Beasts

Yet to the right lay an impressive view. Bald cypress trees, old giants of the new land, and tupelo gum, rooted in primeval times, crowded from the quagmires of the deep swamp onto the river's mud shoals while grey moss streamed from their lofty cones to spread shadows amidst the hollows and provide habitation for those creatures whose design it was to dwell in the sanctuary of darkness . . . a place to be explored safely only by echoes.

Thus the swamp forest stood, as a barrier against a vast country, much as the sand reefs protecting the North Carolina sounds, to which access was known only by the savage . . . and where few of them entered alone except the foolish man and the brave huntsman.

Here lay the kingdom of the Vermine and the wild

Beast—indeed, a rare and pleasant place for them.

The Chowan River Swamp barrier, dotted with scores of islands and pierced by countless sand ridges, was about twenty miles long and in parts four miles wide. Beyond the swamps, to the east, lay the Sand Banks rim buttressed by a flat country dotted here and there by pocosins and extending twenty miles before reaching the wilds of the Great Dismal Swamp, a mysterious morass welling forth water to feed seven swampy rivers and providing exciting tales for no less than four Indian nations.

Wetness of the land had protected most of the forests of this country from fires, and trees of many kinds were permitted to utilize their natural advantages and grow large and productive of masts, nuts and fruits.

In 1586 Ramushonouog, the chief Chowanoke town, peopled by "those who paddle up the back way," was on the north side of the Pochake (Meherrin) River one mile from its confluence with the Chowan. Smaller towns were tucked away in forest clearings to the west and south of these rivers.

Balanced and Plentiful Food Supply

The Chowanokes, largest group of North Carolina's tidewater Indians, had a balanced and plentiful food supply. They depended on hunting, fishing and farming while the coastal peoples relied chiefly on fishing and farming and those further inland, on hunting and farming. The Chowanokes were better fed by far than the more numerous Tuscaroras who ranged over large areas of the North Carolina central plains.

Several sand ridges commencing at the banks of the Chowan River about a mile east of Ramushonouog led eastward into the river pocosins and served as land bridges to this wild country.

Nine miles down stream huntsmen of the tributary

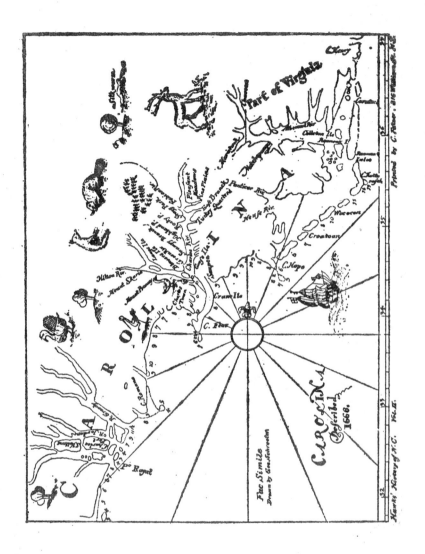

town of Ohanoak had access to the same area by way of a two-mile-long swamp island which would later be given the name of Fort Island, after a legendary Indian fort.

The Indian did not find the swampy eastern side of the Chowan suited for permanent habitation. Deep in these wilds, however, temporary camps were set up for hunting and foraging expeditions. These usually were on the ridges bordering the deep river pocosins, beside the creeks and branches which led from the savannahs and hard bottom pocosins, and upon the high western rim rising from the Dismal Swamp.

The extensive glades of the evergreen white cedar—called juniper by the English settlers—created amazing spectacles in both the Chowan River and the Great Dismal swamps. These were the chief sanctuaries of the deer and thus attracted the interest of the Indian hunter.

One of these glades lay between the sand ridges and the deep peat phase of the Chowan River Pocosin and extended parallel with the river virtually unbroken for about twenty miles. In places this glade, like some of the Dismal Swamp, set up impenetrable barriers against human penetration.

From woodsmen, who cut timber from these glades, it is learned that the tall and slender junipers formed a tightly woven mantle overhead, which generally screened out the sunlight on the brightest days. Below lay the dark corridors, which spread endlessly amidst a tangled maze of fallen trees whose wood was slow to decay.

These sanctuaries provided protection against both the hot summer sun and the cold winter wind with the swamp floor stabilizing the temperature to some extent. Here the deer rested away the bright hours of the day and then ventured out into twilight shadows to browse.

From distribution of artifacts it has been learned that the Indian hunter's camp was pitched most frequently upon those sand ridges which lay nearest to the Chowan Pocosin juniper glades and upon the high land convenient to the glades of the Dismal Swamp.

Chowanokes Traditionally Friendly

The Chowanokes were of Algonquin stock and not so warlike as some of their neighbors. Tradition, however, tells of occasional difficulties both with the Tuscaroras and neighbor Virginia Indians.

A record of friendship with the English begins with the colonists at Fort Raleigh. Some twenty years later reports by Captain John Smith, leader, and William Strachey, secretary of the Virginia Colony at Jamestown, indicate these Indians may have given some of the lost colonists of Roanoke Island temporary sanctuary.

In 1610 Captain Argall was reported leading an expedition from Jamestown "into parts of Chowanock," but no records of his journey have been preserved.

February 1622, twelve years after Argall, John Pory, secretary of the Virginia Colony, made a journey from Jamestown and reported that he "travelled to the South River Chawonock some sixtie miles over land which he found very fruitful and pleasant Country, yielding two harvests in a yeere and found much of the silke grass . . . was kindly used by the people . . ."

The following year Rev. Patrick Copeland, in England, said that Pory "hath trod on good ground, hath past through great forests of Pynes 15 or 16 myle broad and above 60 mile long. . . . On the other side of the River there is a fruitfull Countrye blessed with aboundance of Corne, reaped twise a yeere: above which is the Copper Mines, by all of all places generally affirmed. Hee hath also met with a great deal of silke grasse which growes there."

Pory approached the Chowan River from the northeast and apparently followed an Indian trail along a route which the English would later call "Meherrin Ferry Road." This led from the Nansemond River through northwest Gates County to the Chowan River before crossing over and proceeding one mile to the chief Chowanoke Indian town on the Meherrin River.

Pory mentioned no difficulty of travel along the trail which took him through the large forests dominated by the pine tree.

In 1672 George Fox, the Quaker missionary found travel though the central area of Gates County difficult. From Somerton, Virginia, to Bennetts Creek he traveled "hard through the woods and over many bogs and swamps."

Prior to 1783 J. F. D. Smythe, traveling "around the edge of the Great Dismal Swamp" between Edenton and Suffolk, passed through "a country covered with sand and pines, a country dead flat, infested with swamps, and the land everywhere miserably poor and barren."

Interest in Southern Part of Virginia Grows

Midway the seventeenth century, with political developments in England stimulating immigration to the colonies and extension of the Virginia frontier, interest grew in the Southern part of Virginia. Here, the broad, scantlly explored plains stretched from the coast almost endlessly across fabled savage kingdoms to the mountains and to the mystic South Seas. Nearby lay the beautiful Albemarle country with its many broad waters, fresh black bottom lands, under dominion of friendly Indians.

Development of the Albemarle was of chief consideration when in 1663 and 1665 King Charles II issued grants to the eight Lords Proprietors for a rare sort of governmental experiment in a country which had been represented by many promoters as a virtual Garden of Eden in its natural fruitfulness.

Behind all of this was another dramatic story, that of the development of the rich plantations along the Nansemond River in Virginia. When the good land was taken here the venturesome and hopeful in spirit looked southward to the new frontier.

Sir Thomas Dale opened the way in 1612, even before the Jamestown settlement had been firmly seated, when he explored the Nansemond River to its two main sources. Even then the Indians were heard to say that there lay beyond a black water river leading southward to the Chowan River and the Albemarle Sound.

Indian resistance delayed for a few years English expansion along the Nansemond; but inevitably—and during the decade after 1630—several plantations developed beside the leisurely flowing tidewater river. It was from hence that interest followed a natural course to the Chowan and Albemarle Sound regions.

Yet in between lay a fruitful country made attractive to land seekers by its proximity to Mother Nansemond. Some fourteen miles to the south and upon the western rim of the Great Dismal Swamp good farm land and grazing range for hogs and cattle were found. Tradition states that by 1660 land grants had been made as far south as the Corapeake community in present Gates County, North Carolina.

Meanwhile, a few explorers and fur traders pushed deep into the vast new country and returned with varied reports on the fertility of the land and of the friendliness of the natives. The tide of travelers increased as the Virginia Indian retreated westward and the interest in furs turned chiefly to Carolina. Now more and more Englishmen traced Indian trails to remote villages, and at times they were seen in the familiar Indian log boat journeying upon the waters of the country.

Indian wives were taken, and born from such unions were both children of mixed blood and eventually legends of Indian love. Dr. Bray, who was appointed by the Bishop of London in 1692 to study the state of religion in the colonies, found "Roanoak" (the Albemarle area) to be "peopled with English, intermixed with the native Indians to a great extent." Then at the beginning of the eighteenth century John Lawson observed that the Pasquotank Indians were "the most civilized"—wore clothes, kept cattle and made butter.

Fourteen years after Pory, the pine forests along the Chowan River apparently attracted interest of adventurers, for in 1636 a group of Puritan seamen, fleeing royal persecution, visited the Albemarle Sound area for "sperrits resin." However, the project was a failure. It seems that too many arrived simultaneously for all to make a profit.

In 1646 Governor Sir William Berkley of Virginia — apparently in anticipation of an early development of the region—sent out an expedition against the Indians along the Chowan River, with General Richard Bennett of Nansemond leading a contingent overland and Thomas Dew approaching as far as the mouth of the Wiccacon River in Hertford County by water. By 1707 Dew's son John had settled on the north side of the Meherrin River in present Hertford County.

About 1648 Henry Plumpton of Nansemond County, Thomas Tuke of Isle of Wight and others bought from the Indians "all the Land from Morratuck (Roanoke) River to the mouth of Weyanook (Wiccacon) Creek," with "Cowes, and Oxen, Horses, and Mares, Sheepe and Hogs" offered as part of the provisions.

Nomadic Cattle Herdsmen

Already the century-long story of the Virginia nomadic cattle herdsmen apparently was commencing. Winter grazing in Virginia was poor, and masters of the

Nansemond plantations began sending their servants with herds of livestock southward to forage until spring upon the evergeen reeds and green grass shoots about the pocosins and marshes of the unhabited country between the Chowan River and the Great Dismal swamps.

Crude temporary shelters, less elaborate and comfortable than the Indian cabins, apparently were thrown up as the herdsmen moved their cattle from one grazing area to another. These shelters perhaps were no more than simple lean-tos covered with grass or reeds to break the cold winds; to protect against rain, sleet and snow; and to gather in warmth from the low winter sun and the blazing open log fires.

These people, like the Indian, left the country much as they had found it—wild and unimproved.

War with the Chowanokes

In 1663 the Indians "submitted themselves to the Crown of England under Dominion of the Lords Proprietors," and it seemed that both the savages and the new settlers would be able to share the natural riches of the beautiful country in peace and tranquility.

Strife developed quickly, and by 1666 the Indians and the English were skirmishing with each other. Peace, however, was restored before any great loss of life on either side.

Declared peace did not resolve the problems created by the influx of English settlers. The mounting pressures on the Indian and an exchange of hostilie acts resulted in the outbreak of the Chowanoke War in 1675. This conflagration coincided with and was related to strife upon the Virginia frontier where Nathaniel Bacon and his followers warred against the Indian.

The Indians mustered enough strength to block the Chowan River routes from Virginia and to cut off the trails between the river and the Dismal Swamp. Open only were the difficult trails east of the swamp and the approaches by sea.

The English lost many lives in the wilderness warfare, and the Indians had their towns upon the Meherrin River and its tributaries destroyed.

After about a year, in 1676 the Chowanokes were defeated and removed from their "fruitfull Country" to a reservation without surveyed bounds but estimated to contain twelve square miles, south of Bennetts Creek in Chowan Precinct, a part of Gates County after its formation in 1779.

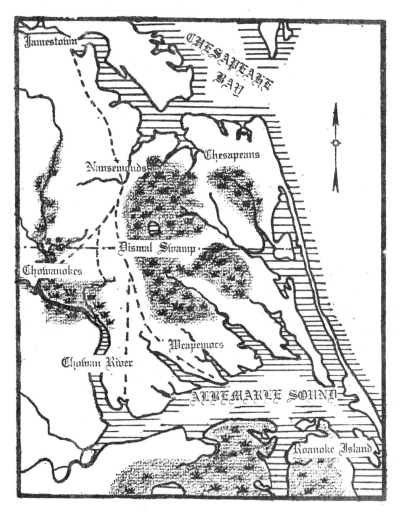

From Jamestown to the Southern Part of Virginia
(Carolina)

Scratching, Fighting Indians

CHAPTER III

Bitter and Insolent

As the eighteenth century opened John Lawson said that the Carolina Indians "never fight one another unless drunk, nor do you ever hear any Scolding amongst them." The Indians, to be sure, marveled at the Europeans whom they found to be "always rangling and uneasy." They wondered that "they do not go out of this World, since they are so uneasy and discontented in it."

Lawson's representation of the noble savage applied to the organized and disciplined Indians of nations like the Tuscarora who had not been subjugated by the English.

However, after the Carolina and Virginia Indian wars wrecked the nations of the east those survivors who did not join other nations broke up into bitter and insolent groups.

Such was the fate of the loosely - knit bands of Indians which moved onto the vacated Chowanoke old fields and utilized their old hunting and fishing grounds. These people were called Meherrins by the English because they had come down Pochake (Meherrin) River from the traditional Meherrin Indian country.

Their story, however, extended back much further. For the most part, they were the survivors of broken warlike Indian nations of Virginia, Maryland and Pennsylvania, with the Susquehannahs being the more numerous among them.

The Susquehannahs had taken up the tomahawk

when pressures mounted against their villages upon water-courses of the Maryland and Pennsylvania border. In reprisal of a bloody massacre, Virginia and Maryland forces pursued them into the wilderness, and one Major Trueman beseiged them eight months in a fort at the head of the Potomac River.

One night, however, the trapped Indians broke through the main guard and most of them escaped. They vanished into the wilderness, moved southward skirting the heads of several rivers, and made their way to "Old Sapponie Town" on the Meherrin River near present Lawrenceville, Virginia. The Sapponies drove them down the river to Tarrora Creek, from whence the Jennetos, a native Meherrin group, spurred them on their journey to the vacated Chowanoke old fields upon the new English frontier in the old county of Albemarle in Carolina.

One group of the stragglers settled on Bennetts Creek in Chowan Precinct beside the Chowan Indian reservation, on a "Neck of land afterwards called Maherrin Neck because these Indians came down the Maherrin River."

At various intervals, other groups moved into the country to the west of the Chowan River, and eventually they became so numerous that the resources of the country were strained to provide them natural support.

The English promptly found these impoverished and miserable people to be moody, disrespectful of English property rights and a threat to the general peace. An unpleasant story of their struggle for survival commenced.

Indian Allegiance Disputed

Stress was added to the sorry English-Indian relations by embroilment of North Carolina and Virginia in their bitter dividing line dispute which would drag on unsettled until the joint survey of 1728. Involved were both allegiance of the Indians and a 20-mile-wide strip of land lying east and west between Wiccacon Creek and Nottoway River. The dispute grew so bitter that at times the area was regarded as being outside of both governments.

Neither Virginia nor North Carolina appointed justices for the area, and public officials conceded that, in addition to the troublesome Indian renegades, lawless Englishmen moved into it and were able to do much as they pleased.

As the eighteenth century opened a few Englishmen were taking up and seeking to settle lands to the west of the Chowan River, and the hindrance caused by the Meherrin Indian presence proved a great annoyance to the Carolina government. For a quarter of a century correspondence between the two states is filled with a series of complaints regarding the Indian problem.

In 1703 Deputy Governor Henderson Walker observed that these Indians "do daily Commit great injuries to the inhabitants of that province by destroying their stocks and burning their timber and houses . . ."

After a "barbarous assault" upon Lewis Williams over a land dispute south of Catherines Creek, Coll. Thomas Pollock raised "sixty armed men" and "sett upon the Maherine Indian town" and in the heat of summer held thirty six prisoners without water in a small fort two days. As a show of force and determination he pulled down some of their cabins at "Little Town" and promised to burn the rest and destroy their corn if they did not remove.

Virginia was shocked by the hostile action and protested it as a threat to the security of both colonies. The treatment, it was feared, might bring "forreigne Indians to Revenge their wrongs."

The Indian stragglers at Little Town upon Caterines Creek, however, yielded to this show of determination and moved to the main town north of the Meherrin River. It then was found that removal of their habitations alone was not adequate; for "they being still mischievious by order of Coll Pollock brought in the chief of them before the Govr & Council and they were then ordered by the Government never to appear on the south side of the Meherrin."

The threat of a general Indian conflagration during the Tuscarora War prompted Virginia and North Carolina to lay aside temporarily their feud over the Meherrins. These Indians were kept neutral although it was known that their sympathies lay with the Tuscaroras and they were suspected of supplying them with arms and ammunition.

The Chowan Indians, now somewhat acclimated to the English presence, allied themselves with the English. They sent their fighting men upon several expeditions against the Tuscaroras while the Meherrins, as Pollock charged, continued to kill and drive back stock of the English south of the Meherrin River.

When one of the Meherrin stragglers was captured by a ranger and taken to one John Beverly's upon the Chowan River one mile below its confluence with the Meherrin River, "In a little time about eighteen of the Meherrin Indians came upe, most of them armed and forced them to lett loose the indian they had taken, giveing them threatening and abusive language . . ."

Soon after the Tuscarora War a serious illness among the Meherrins struck them a weakening blow. Large numbers died and the survivors scurried up the Meherrin River several miles from their accursed town.

By 1723 both the Meherrin and Nansemond Indians, at the mouth of Indian (Buckhorn) Creek eight miles up the Chowan River from the Meherrin, were complaining that "divers persons, under pretense of Grants from the Government of North Carolina" were settling upon their cleared grounds.

Then in 1727 the Catawba Indians, traditional enemies of the Meherrins' marauding Iroquois kinsmen of New

York, struck a mortal blow. Fourteen persons were killed in a surprise raid, and the frightened survivors fled to the east of the Chowan River and sought sanctuary beside the English who were then establishing plantations in the Scratch Hall pine barrens.

One year later a group of these Meherrins appeared before the dividing line commissioners with the complaint they were being "hardly used" by the English. Their plight appeared quite similar to that of the broken bands of Tuscaroras which a few years earlier were reported to be "living like beasts without habitation, and without provisions than what the woods afforded."

By 1729, however, some of these harassed Indians were back at their old town on the Meherrin River complaining of new encroachments by the English. With the jurisdiction over the area settled by the dividing line survey, a reservation containing less than four square miles was laid out in the fork of the Meherrin and Chowan rivers by North Carolina and the Indians given rights to it as long as they should occupy the land.

Edward Moseley's 1733 map of Carolina shows Meherrin Indian habitations in the Scratch Hall area of Chowan Precinct (Gates County) and Meherrin Indian Town at the traditional Meherrin River site.

Battle Against Extermination

Meanwhile, the Chowan Indians, waging a battle against extermination, continued at their reservation south of Bennetts Creek. Repeatedly, they petetioned the Colonial Council to protect their reservation by having it surveyed and its boundaries definitely established. By 1707 the reservation was reduced to six square miles, and in 1720 Chief John Hoyter informed the Colonial Council "several of the white people are continually intrudeing upon their Land and the same hath never been so determinedly bounded and ascertained pursuant to the grants made to them by the government." Finally, in 1723, upon instruction from the Council, the surveyor general of the colony "laid out for the Tuscarora Indians and the Chowans fifty three thousand acres of land."

This action, however, did not stem the decay of the Chowan nation. Large numbers of their young people joined the nations of the western frontiers, and others were captured by enemy Indians and sold into slavery. The Chowans had lost heavily in both men and possessions while aiding the English in the Tuscarora War. Chief Hoyter explained that his warriors had "been upon Eight Expeditions agt the Indian Enemy in this province," and that "they suffered Considerable loss in their plantations & Stocks loosing Seveanty five head of hoggs a Mare & Colt their Corne destroyed by all wch & ye wearing out of their clothes they are reduced to great poverty."

The Rev. Thomas Newman said in 1722 that all the Indians in the old County of Albemarle did not exceed 300 fighting men and that "they live in 2 towns by themselves very quiet and peaceable." He observed that "as to ye converting them to ye Christian Faith it is a thing that I almost despair of ever seeing effected whilst among them."

The population of the once strong nation of many warriors had been reduced to about 250, and seventeen years later in 1731 Governor Burrington reported their number had dwindled to less than twenty families.

In 1733 the Colonial Council gave its permission for the Chowans to be incorporated into the Tuscarora nation then occupying the Indian Woods reservation in Bertie County, but there is no evidence that any of their number joined their old enemy.

In 1734 the Carolina government granted a petition by the Chowans for permission to sell part of their lands when the Indians said that they had grown too few in umber to cultivate all their holdings. Signing the petition as chief men were Thomas Hoyter, James Bennet, Charles Beazley and Jeremiah Pushing.

Thomas Hoyle was mentioned as king of the nation in 1712 and John Hitau was a chief man in 1722.

Deterioration apparently accelerated, for by 1752 the Chowan nation was reduced to a few families and most of their land had been taken by encroachment or sold.

The Meherrins now were scattered among the English. Some remained in western Gates County, and by 1752 a "mere handful" preserving nation status had moved away from the Meherrin River westward along Potecasi Creek. Bishop Spargenberg observed, "It would seem that a curse were resting upon them and oppressing them."

Tradition states that the last Indian settlement in the Hall area of Gates County was a palisade encampment upon the large Chowan River Pocosin island which came to be known as Fort Island. People of full Indian blood lived upon this island until a few decades before the Civil War.

By the Revolution, however, the Chowan, Meherrin and Nansemond Indians, for all practical purposes, had lost their tribal identity. Left were only scattered clannish-like groups gradually being assimilated into the white and Negro populations.

The English, now in possession of the Indian's lands, also had their language enriched by addition of many Indian words; and English lore and literature were brightened by addition of Indian traditions, myths and legends.

Legend of Batz' Grave

One of the more beautiful Chowan legends is a story of an English hunter's tragic love for a Chowanoke Indian princess.

It was said that before Carolina was cut off from Virginia and made into a separate colony one Jesse Batz came southward to the beautiful country of the Chowanokes.

These friendly and hospitable Indians permitted him to hunt and trap their large forests which lay to the east of the Chowan River and north of the Albemarle Sound.

Batz was admired by the Chowanokes for his fearlessness, and they happily had him join them on their hunts.

One early day of his sojourn in this country of great rivers and wildernesses he saw the beautiful Princess Kickawana, daughter of King Kilkanoo of the Chowanokes. He loved her at first sight, and she returned his love.

Batz proved his bravery when he joined the Chowanokes in defensive battle against invading Pamunkey and his Indian braves. He engaged this warrior in hand-to-hand combat, made him prisoner, and helped to drive his followers back into Virginia. The grateful Chowanokes promptly adopted him into their tribe and honored him with the name Secotan, meaning Great White Eagle.

The love between Batz and the Indian princess brought them unblemished happiness, until one night as she paddled her canoe from the mainland for Kaola Island a violent thunderstorm swept the face of the Albemarle. . . .

"The wind was high and the clouds were dark,
And the boat returned no more."

Batz was so grief-stricken that he never again left his island home. He sorrowed for the Indian maiden there until his death. He was buried on Kaola Island which story tellers remembered as Batz' Grave.

Other storms have eaten away Kaola spreading its hallowed soil over the Albemarle Sound.

Purchase on Fort Island

Tradition states that the first Eure who came from England settled first on Bennetts Creek near the present site of Gatesville.

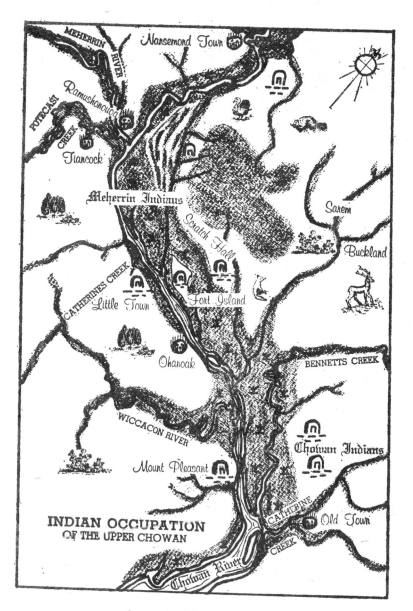

from 1586 to 1729

At that time no Englishmen were living in the western part of present Gates County. This area, comprised of a band of pocosins and sand ridges upon the Chowan River, was occupied by the Indians. These Indians, however, were on friendly terms with the new settlers, and Eure went into their country often to hunt deer and turkeys.

One day, while exploring a new hunting range, Eure came upon an island in the large river pocosin. It was more than two miles long, had rich black earth, and only a narrow strip of pocosin lay between it and the great river.

Although Eure had patented a good tract of land and established a plantation on deep-water Bennetts Creek, he was so struck by the advantages of the pocosin island that he determined that he must have a parcel of it. He discovered to his dismay that the Indians valued it as much as he and they would accept nothing which he offered in exchange.

However, when he came again to Fort Island he drove the two white horses which he had brought with him from England. The Indians were fascinated by the beauty of the horses and began offering to swap their prized possessions for them. Eure saw his opportunity and bargained the horses for the coveted land.

It is said that Eure's purchase has remained in the Eure family to this day.

A second version of the legend states that an English settler swapped a white horse with the Indians for a large tract of pine forest which included the "Grape Vine Farm" south of Sarem Creek near the original site of Scratch Hall where another legend claims a band of fighting and scratching Indians lived.

PART 2

The Wild Frontier

CHAPTER IV

Indian Trails and Pine Barrens

No less than three Indian trails connected the Nansemond River country of Virginia with the Chowan River and the Albemarle Sound areas of North Carolina.

One of these trails passed through extensive pine barrens of western Gates County and perhaps was traveled by John Pory upon his 1622 journey to the lower river Chowanoke. A second followed the western rim of the Great Dismal Swamp through extensive pine barrens of old Perquimans Precinct. A third passed through branches and across bogs into the central part of Gates County to Bennetts Creek near Gatesville, the way seemingly taken by George Fox in 1672.

These trails were like thin ribbons which moved about the carpet of shadows laid by great trees without making a perceptible mark on the primeval forest. For these, at best, were simple narrow ways suited to foot travel. They bent their courses in quest of natural advantages—the high and open ridge woodlands—and avoided obstructions—thickets, bogs and pocosins.

Pory found the pine barrens a prominent feature of the country. A long-bodied species, which had a dense symmetrical cone with spindly needle-leaves shooting in clusters like quills of the porcupine, dominated the highland forest. A lean scrawny species, which combed the wind with its ragged cones of short clustering needles, rose rugged and loney from the grasses and thickets of the wet bottom lands.

Frequent incidence of pocosins, branches and savannahs broke the monotony of the forests to some extent; but the country was so vast and wild that the stranger without a guide was in danger of going astray and becoming lost. In 1704 Rev. James Blair, a missionary for the Society for the Propogation of the Gospel, said "there is no possibility for a stranger to find his way" in the back - country from the Albemarle waterways, "for if he once goes astray (it being such a desert country) it is great hazard if he ever finds his way again."

Confusing Natural Beauty

The natural beauty of the country was admired by newcomers. Complimentary John Lawson left one of the more favorable and interesting descriptions of early eighteenth century Carolina.

The great savannahs, largely to the south of the Albemarle, extended for several miles without trees and were "adorned by Nature with a pleasant Verdue, and beautiful Flowers, frequent in no other Places, yielding abundance of Herbage for Cattle, Sheep, and Horses."

The whole of the unsettled country—inhabited by the birds, insects, vermine, beasts and reptiles—at times was dominated by confusing noises as well as the cherry and pleasant ones. Lawson explained that one of the two frogs was

"the Bull-Frog, so called, because he lows exactly like the Beast, which make the Stranger wonder (when by the side of a Marsh) what is the matter, for they hear the frogs low and can see no cattle . . ."

After passing through densely canopied forests the stranger was likely to relate fastastic seeming stories. The

Bald Eagle deceived him into believing the country was inhabited by flying sows and pigs. For, explained Lawson, this bird

"is an Artist at stealing young Pigs, which Prey he carries alive to his Nest, at which time the poor Pig makes such a Noise over Head, that Strangers have thought there were Flying Sows and Pigs in that country."

The large owls, which made their nests in hollows of the pocosin trees and were known to the settlers as "hooting" or "booting" owls, seemed to delight in confusing the newcomers. Lawson explained that this bird

"is as big as a middling Goose, and has a prodigious Head. They make a fearful Hollowing in the Night-time, like a Man, whereby they often make Strangers lose their way in the Woods."

The Indian was confused by the mysteries of the distant country. Lawson was told by the savage

"that on a Lake of Water towards the Head of Neus-River, there haunts a Creature which frightens them all from Hunting thereabouts. They say he is of the Colour of a Panther, but cannot run up Trees; and that there abides with him a Creature like an Englishman's Dog, which runs faster than he can, and gets his Prey for him. They add that there is no other way to avoid him but by running up a Tree."

Illustrating the hazard of the Great Dismal Swamp, William Byrd recited a story as told him by a Mr. Wilson, an eastern borderer. A North Briton, seemingly spurred by curiosity, went

"a long way into this great Desert, as he called it . . . but he having no Compass, nor seeing the Sun for several Days Together, wander'd about till he was almost famisht; but at last he bethought himself of a Secret his Countrymen make use of to Pilot themselves in a Dark day.

"He took a fat Louse out of his Collar, and expos'd it to the open day on a Piece of White Paper, which he brought along with him for his Journal. The poor Insect having no Eye-lids, turn'd himself about till he found the Darkest Part of the Heavens, and so made the best of his way towards the North. By this Direction he Sterr'd himself Safe out, and the distresses he underwent, that no mortall Since has been hardy enough to go upon the like dangerous Discovery."

The many thuckleberry slashes lying between the Chowan River Pocosin and the Dismal Swamp harbored a large number of wolves which, as a destroyer of livestock, became an annoyance to the planter. The wolf was too timid to attack a man or a dog, but he made the nights wakeful with his wierd cries. On one occasion, said Byrd,

"We were entertained this Night with the Yell of a Whole Family of Wolves, in which we cou'd distinguish the Treble, Tenor and Bass, very clearly. These Beasts of Prey kept pretty much upon our Track, being tempted by the garbage of the Creatures we'd kill'd every day; for which we were serenaded with their Shrill Pipes almost every Night. This beast is not so untamable as the Panther, but the Indians know how to gentle their Whelps, and use them about their cabins instead of dogs."

The panther, a great destroyer of the planter's stock, was the most feared and the most storied of the wild creatures. He purred like a cat and "hollows like a Man in the Woods when killed," said Lawson. When in extreme hunger he was ready to match his agility against the strong arms of the bear, and he was never known the loser. Traditional stories from the old Albemarle area and especially about the Dismal Swamp, represent the panther as holding ill feelings against man and constantly seeking to lead him astray to perish in the deep woods. From the early days of the colony it was customary for men to let their presence be known by hollering as they passed through the woods. The panther, claims tradition, imitatated them. It was customary for him to dig a hole in the ground, place his mouth in it and cry to make it seem that he was afar; then to thrust his head upward and cry to make it seem that he was very near.

Common were the stories of narrow escape from the panther's treachery; and added to these is the conjecture that many of the people who mysteriously disappeared had been lured into the barrens by him and perished. From the Dismal Swamp border comes this story:

Once a boy became lost in the forest and wandered much of the night. Before daybreak he heard the cry of a panther, but being acquainted with the noises of the wild animals of the country he recognized the treachery. Thus he boldly walked away from the cry and soon found himself in familiar country and safety.

Timid and Marvelous Creatures

The deer, the chief prey of the panther and the Indian hunter, occupied the country in large numbers. The tender shoots of shrubs, the grasses, masts and acorns all took turns at supplying his constant food requirements.

Abundant and varied foods also supported large populations of other common animals and birds.

The traveler grew accustomed to their frequent appearance along his way. Often he was entertained by their

Beastes of Carolina — from Lawson's History

chattering talk and varied songs.

The black bear quickly was recognized as a marvelous glutton. He stuffed himself with masts, nuts and berries, and when other foods grew scarce he ventured near the planter's habitation to steal a pig, lamb or calf. He also went fishing upon the small streams. Lawson admired his art at catching the herring fish.

"They sit by the Creek-sides, (which are very narrow) where the fish run in, and there they take them up as fast as it is possible they can dip their Paws into the Water."

The bear had a bad habit of destroying food bearing trees. He would gnaw off limbs of the chestnut and oak, break off the limbs of the brittle bowl gum and finish his meal of nuts and berries on the ground.

He made the planter angry by his wasteful habits, destroying more roasting ear corn than he ate and rooting sweet potatoes from the ground to waste.

Clouds of blackbirds and pigeons wheeled into the pocosins to roost in the gallberry and thuckleberry thickets, from whence the wildcat stole them when he was not busy thieving the planter's pigs and lambs.

The long-nosed, long-tusk piney-wood type hog had gone wild as had some of the strays from the small black cattle which years before had been introduced to this pocosin country from the neighboring Virginia colony.

Also quite common were the many smaller animals which would become delightfully personified in the folk lore and fable—the persimmon-loving opossum, the fishing raccoon, the smart dark swamp rabbit, the scheming grey highland bunny, the tireless nut-cutting grey squirrel of the hardwood forests and the phantom red fox squirrel, the dark coated otter, the cypress and juniper swampdwelling muskrat and mink, the mischievious beaver whose dams choked up the back-lands, and the curious and cunning fox.

Turkeys of three types—yellow, green, black—grew fat upon the acorns. Tradition states that if undisturbed, they would range an area every seventh day.

The noble birds—adding life to the forest and food for the table — were the phesant, woodcock, snipe, quail, grouse, dove, lark, oriole, duck and goose. Also there were the odd characters, the owl and crow, and the hawk in great numbers; the martin, sentinel of the plantation; and the many migratory and lesser birds.

Varied and Mysterious Forests

The varied forest which rolled over the sand ridges and across the great pocosins to the eastern side of the Chowan River must have been an awe-inspiring primeval wilderness, somewhat like the Great Dismal Swamp. Even today parts of this forest has resisted significant change.

Here, sand ridge fingers provided avenues into dark regions which at the end of the nineteenth century was about as isolated as when they were visited by the first settlers.

Soil variety and the water table of the country east of the Chowan River Pocosin to the Dismal Swamp produced most types of trees common to eastern Carolina. The cypress, juniper and gum dominated the swamps and the pine and oak covered the sand ridges while other trees thrived in their places of vantage.

The traveler found the willow weeping mournfully beside the creeks and observed that the laurel and myrtle sought out the nearby low grounds. Upon the rising ground rose the proud sycamore, with its mottled bark, which tradition said no squirrel would attempt to climb lest he ride a carpet of loose bark to earth. The great poplar or tulip, which in season gloried in its white flowers, stood in occasional groves. The dogwood, which bequeathed its flower both to North Carolina and Virginia, spread over most of the highland where its white petals set stages for the dancing fairies and told both the Indian and Englishman the annual schools of shad and herring fish were on their way upriver to spawn in the tributary creeks.

The long leaf pine of the sand ridges would make turpentine barons of some of the settlers and poor people of many of the laborers. Oaks thrived as a large family, with the white and red varieties more common, to provide materials for coopers to ply their trade in staves and barrels. The lesser varieties included the black, Spanish, chestnut, scaly bark, and the evergreen water oak.

Common to the country also were the ash, elm, beech, birch, sassafras, persimmon, locust, hicory, black walnut, maple, chestnut and chinquapin.

Vines added to the forest variety—from the sweet-flowered honeysuckle which the story tellers said the Lord had forbidden the Sunday-working honey bee to suck, to creepers which climbed to the tallest trees and periodically decking them with flowers and forming mysterious fairy bowers, and the four varieties of grapes which made harbors of the trees.

Repulsive and Noxious Creatures

The black snake lorded over the sand ridges where he fed upon hordes of insects, small birds and rodents.

The poisonous cottonmouth moccosin— or perchance the Devil in disguise — lay silently beside the pathway as it descended into the damps of the pocosin.

The traveler viewed the snakes of the great pocosins as a "disgustful" sight. When, in the 1770's, J. F. D. Smythe crossed over the Chowan into the eastern part of Hertford (now Gates) County, he saw large numbers of snakes "lying upon logs and fallen trees" where they were "basking themselves in the sun." The "marsh, morass, or pocosin" was found to abound with the "disgustful creatures."

The moccosin was "as large as the rattle-snake, but thicker, shorter, and destitute of rattles." This snake, it was said, bit without warning and was "equally poisonious and fatal," while some people said it was more so.

The moccosin was "beautifully speckled, just in the same manner as the rattle-snake, though they appear duller, the colours of each being the same, but those of the moccosins not so bright; for the similitude between them is not so very strong, that these are generally reckoned the female rattle-snake, by the more ignorant inhabitants."

Although the bite of either of the snakes meant "certain death," the inhabitants were under "very slender apprehensions" from them and seemed to dread them no more than other snakes.

Snakebite Remedy Wins Slave Freedom

Smythe stated that "a remedy of efficacy" for the bite of these snakes had been discovered—"equal quantities of the juices of horehound and plantain, administered internally, largely and frequently, and poultices of the bruised plant applied to the wound."

"It was a poor negroe slave that first discovered this valuable sovereign remedy; and the assembly, or parliament of North Carolina, rewarded him with his freedom and two hundred pounds for divulging it. . . .

"Notwithstanding this plain and simple remedy may be readily obtained, and easily administered by the most ignorant, as both horehound and plantain grow spontaneously near almost every house and in most places where the land has been cleared of woods; yet the knowledge of this great benefit to

[36]

be derived from them has extended but very little, occasioned by the small intercourse, and very limited communication there is in general between the thinly and distantly scattered inhabitants of this widespread country. . . ."

Legendary Snake Creek

The multitudes of snakes found in the Chowan River pocosins apparently account for the fable of legendary Snake Creek, which is still a part of local lore.

Snake Creek is described as a narrow inky-black stream which "snakes" it way eastward from the Chowan River into the bogs of the great pocosin forest. Along the way the gum and cypress trees take turns at completing a leafy archway overhead while in the intermittent splotches of light long streamers of grey moss lap at the bosom of the stream. The creek has no real end. It just wanders into morasses beyond serpent-infested water grass thickets.

No one will tell you where Snake Creek is to be found, for none of the local inhabitants seem to know. All the mapped creeks have other names.

Yet everyone knows the chief characteristics of Snake Creek. Tradition has explained that snakes are to be found anywhere — along its jungle-like shorelines, in the frequent clumps of grasses and bushes, upon fallen tree trunks, in branches outstretched arm-like over the water . . . and everywhere there is a patch of spring sunshine or a mottled summer shadow.

The snakes of Snake Creek take it upon themselves to rule the place. Noisy people are strictly forbidden. If insulted by their clamor the snakes resort to unnerving delights — slither from an overhanging limb into the boats or gather into droves and swim from their resting places in pursuit of the intruders.

The firing of a gun upon Snake Creek is a declaration

of hostility and the guest who acts so rashly must be ready for a hasty departure.

Fishermen say that any one of the several pocosin creeks along the Chowan River rightfully could be called Snake Creek — Mud Creek, Barnes Creek, Buckhorn Creek, Sarem Creek and others.

A possible explanation of the mysterious creek is heard when a fisherman in provincial lingo says he is going down to "Snake Creek" when he means "Snaky Mud Creek," "Snaky Barnes Creek," and so on.

When Time Stood Still

In 1857 Port Crayon described a spring day on the upper Chowan River and left the impression time had stood as motionless as the river's glassy surface during a calm. He observed:

"Buzzards sailed in lazy majesty athwart the blue sky, and the mud-colored terrapins basked luxuriously upon convenient drift logs, motionless as stones, until the waves from the passing boat rolled them over and unceremoniously plumped them into the water. But this paradise seemed as yet untenanted by the human race."

The No-Man's-Land

CHAPTER V

Basis for Settlement

Although a few scattered habitations and plantations were established in several parts of present Gates County before or soon after the coming of the Carolina Proprietary, there was no large growth in population for one-half a century.

For, most of the Virginians looking southward and Englishmen coming directly from the Mother Country preferred the country about the Albemarle waterways. Here the Albemarle Sound and its broad tributary rivers provided both "a noble Prospect" for the plantations and convenience of water travel and commerce.

By contrast, the country lying between the Chowan River and the Great Dismal Swamp had but few places with river or navigable creek frontage; and within a few years the greater part of it had fallen within the Virginia-Carolina disputed area.

After one-half of a century had slipped past, the eighteenth century opened with altered circumstances which caused the land to be taken up rapidly. This once shunned country experienced a steady development up to the Revolutionary War.

The pine forests, which had been given special mention by Pory, encouraged settlement of large areas of the country. In 1705 the English Parliament instituted bounty payments for colonial naval stores, and within a few years the sand ridges, unsuited for agriculture but productive of the long leaf pine, were being taken up. By 1750 the many hard-bottom pocosins and low-lying ridges were providing oak trees needed for the production of barrel staves. At the same time shingles were being produced from white cedar and cypress trees of the deep swamps.

The Carolina pine was a splendid producer of tar and turpentine, even exceeding the production of the Virginia species, conceded William Byrd. This capability of the long leaf pine, within a few decades, would make the Sand Banks area of Gates County famed for its tar, pitch and turpentine. At the same time shingle manufacture would grow into an important industry upon the Dismal Swamp while the broad pocosin-pocketed expanse between the swamps would be found most suited for establishing of plantations.

Other factors accelerated the country's growth. Defeat of the Tuscarora Indians in 1713 removed the last major Indian threat in eastern Carolina, and a large new tide of settlers, chiefly from Virginia, created a scarcity of land. Before this interest had fully materialized, the turbulent Proprietary governmental experiment came to a close, and North Carolina became a crown colony like its neighbors.

The central area seemingly was becoming well populated by 1712. In June that year Rev. Giles Rainsford, a minister for the Society for the Propogation of the Gospel, "preached at one Mr. Garrets the upper end of Chowan (later Gates) but had such numbers that I was obliged to go under a large mulberry tree." There were enough children for a Mr. Marshburn to keep a school "at Sarum on the frontiers of Virginia" which was open both to English and Indian students. The Sarem site was known as Indian town in 1719 when an Episcopal Chapel, the first in the area, was established there. In the 1750's Sarem was a preaching station for Rev. Clement Hall of Edenton.

Then by 1728 the Virginia - Carolina border area was

densely settled, with habitations being located less than a mile apart. It is noted that the dividing line commissioners mentioned eighteen homesteads within the sixteen miles between the Dismal Swamp and Somerton Creek.

Disorderly Flock to No-Man's-Land

Most of the country had fallen within the No-Man's-Land created by the Virginia-Carolina dividing line dispute. That part to the north and west of Bennetts Creek became a part of Hertford County when that county was established in 1759. This and the upper portions of Chowan and Perquimans counties were made into Gates County in 1779.

Virginia admitted to making land grants in the border area prior to the survey. North Carolina grew more confident of its ownership and began to make grants over Virginia's protests.

In 1692 Thomas Milner had found "Bennett's Creek, Buckland, Sarum &c," lay out of Virginia but "Summerton" was in.

In 1714 Governor Spotswood of Virginia observed that to the No-Man's-Land "loose and disorderly people daily flock," and contemporary reports suggest that among these people were free Negroes, run-away slaves, debtors and convicts. These people, like the Indian, were quite ready to use the king's lands without bothering to take out patents.

The sanctuary continued for a number of years, for in 1728 Lieutenant Governor William Gooch of Virginia said that the dividing line controversy had been a great inconvenience to both the Virginia and Carolina governments and "no small detriment to private persons, whose debtors found a safe retreat within the Bounds in dispute, where the law of neither Province could reach them ..."

The notorious liberties taken began to come to an end

[41]

in 1728 when the dividing line survey placed the twenty-mile-wide disputed area between the mouths of the Nottoway River and Wiccacon Creek in North Carolina.

The Carolina commission observed that taken in east of the Blackwater River were "a very great quantity of Lands and Numerous Families that before had been under Verginia of which the time would not admit to take an Exact account but computed about one hundred Thousand acres and above Three hundred Tythables . . ."

The survey prompted Byrd to write his satirical dividing line histories which depict life on the border. The carefree settlers, he said, were "Apprehensive lest their Lands Should be taken into Virginia. In that case they must have submitted to some Sort of Order and Government; whereas, in N Carolina, every One does what seems best in his own Eyes."

Intercolonial Ways Opened

By the middle of the eighteenth century several intercolonial roads passed between the Great Dismal Swamp and the Chowan River Swamp barriers to the Albemarle Sound and the growing new settlements south of the Chowan and Roanoke rivers.

In 1758 the first post route in North Carolina ran from Suffolk, Virginia, to Edenton. Tradition states it passed through Somerton, Sarem and Pipkin's Inn before continuing to Edenton. From here it crossed over the Albemarle Sound to Mackeys and continued south. Another route from the Albemarle area to Virginia passed through the pine barrens along the western rim of the Dismal Swamp.

Livestock drovers, plying a spectacular form of trade during most of the eighteenth century, traveled two or more routes which took them through the swamps and pine barrens of the western part of Gates County. As eastern Carolina filled up with people so did it with hogs, cattle, horses and sheep. By 1733 as many as fifty thousand hogs were driven into Virginia, and interest in livestock continued widespread throughout the colonial period. In 1755 Alexander Shaw said "Every proprietor of ever so small a piece of land, raises some Indian Corn and sweet potatoes, and breeds some hoggs and a calf or two . . ."

The drovers avoided the long ferry crossings of the Albemarle Sound and the lower rivers. They found it to their advantage to take shorter upstream crossings.

After Bertie Precinct was carved from Chowan in 1722 ferries began to span the upper Chowan River and connect the southwest side with ways into Virginia. That year Henry Baker obtained permission to operate a ferry "near Meherring," and two years afterwards Baker was complaining that Col. William Maule, in violation of the two-mile rule, was keeping a ferry "at or near the same place" where Baker had been authorized to keep his. These accomodations, like John Cheshire's Ferry established nearby on the Meherrin River in 1718, apparently were chiefly to serve the intercolonial trade.

No ferry accomodations were available in 1710 when Philip Ludwell and Nathaniel Harrison, Virginia commissioners, and John Lawson and Edward Moseley, Carolina commissioners, traversed the area seeking to settle the boundary dispute. From Beverly's at the mouth of the Meherrin River they "crossed Chawan in a wretched Canoe to Maherink Landing which is on the North-East side of Chawan and is about 2 miles up the river from Beverlys, there being no firm land nearer." From there the travelers followed the old Indian trail to Edward Barnes, from whence it passed through the pine barrens into Virginia.

The heavy livestock traffic into Virginia assuredly was a big encouragement to construction of the long causeways from the ferry crossings through the Chowan River pocosins. The first causeway seems to have been built at Beverly's to save most of the two-mile ferry trip to "Maherink Landing."

Soon after 1740 Theophilus Pugh opened a ferry at Edward Outlaw's Landing on the Chowan at or near the site of the town of Winton, and construction of a three-mile-long causeway was required. After Pugh's death the property was acquired by John Cotton and the name changed to Cotton's Ferry.

Increase in ferry patronage coincided with the development of the country to the south, for two other ferries with long causeways were opened. Before the Revolution a ferry was in operation at Barfield's Landing two miles down the Chowan from Cotton's, and by 1800 Brown's Ferry eight miles down stream from Cotton's at Sarem Creek placed Gates Court House within five miles of Hertford County. This route, with three miles of puncheoned causeway, gave Gatesville a port on the Chowan River and was remembered in tradition as a toll road.

The several ways took travelers through the strange country of sharp contrasts—great swamps, savannahs, sand barrens, plantations; poverty, plenty.

They saw just enough of the isolated Gates County countrysides and heard just enough about the culture of the people to stir the imagination, and this apparently led to the creation of fables. It also was inevitable that this quiet and easy going country should seem more quaint and provincial as the colonial period retired into history and its manners and customs continued on.

Health and Habits of People

CHAPTER VI

Pleasant Clime, Intemperate People

The old County of Albemarle in Carolina may have had a healthful and pleasant climate and possessed the natural advantages for making an easy living, as some writers represented it; but the greater part of the people, ruled by the rigors of the frontier rather than personal or governmental discipline, showed little profit in health and beauty. It seems that frequently "happiness" was achieved by excessive indulgences.

There were some execptions — but very rare ones. Where there was one man who possessed the industry and discipline necessary to increase his wealth and live in dignity amidst a balanced plenty, there were ten or more men who abused their freedoms and adopted sloathful and intemperate habits.

Thus here, where most free men had about equal opportunity for personal advancement, each one seemed to prosper in the measure of his ambition and industry. Men began to fall into classes of their own tastes and making.

The country became peopled by men of various sorts, and they provided ample examples for travelers and writers to portray it as the kind of place they would have it to be. Such literary liberties were taken as is evidenced by the various favorable and unfavorable representations.

As the eighteenth century opened John Lawson found the natives to be "straight, clean-limbed People," their children seldom sufferers from rickets and other distempers, and their women "often fair . . . well featured" and possessing "charming Eyes which sets them off to Advantage."

Then along came William Byrd who said that while the Virginia-Carolina borderers made an easy living they "pay dear in their Persons, for they are devoured by musketas all Summer and have Agues every Spring and Fall, which Corrupt all the Juices of their Bodies, give them a cadaverous complexion, and besides a lazy, creeping Habit, which they never get rid of." The yaws came upon them from over indulgence in swine's flesh, and the gout made mockery of intemperate habits by crippling some.

A few years before the Revolution, J. F. D. Smythe said that people of the pine barrens southwest of the Chowan River appeared ignorant, churlish, "sordid and mean, being of a sallow complexion and yellowish hue, almost as tawney as mulattoes, with the smoak of the light-wood . . . cloathed in cotton rags, that had been once dyed some colour, and all enveloped in dirt and nastiness."

Little Female Beauty

Byrd found little female beauty in a gathering of the border inhabitants, except for "Majr. Alston's Daughter, who is said to be no niggard of it." To the east of the Great Dismal Swamp Timothy Jones' daughter had "a Yielding Sandy Complexion," another young woman was "a Tallow-faced wench," and a mulatto girl was represented as "a Dark Angel" with a deep copper complexion, fine shape and regular features which "made her appear like a Statue in bronze done by a masterly hand." To the west of the swamp at Thomas Speight's "We saw 2 truss Damsels stump about very Industriously, that were handsome enough on a March." Their mother, by comparison, was a loose woman addicted to drink. A "Neat Land-lady" was found at Thomas Parker's.

A few years after Byrd, Mark Catesby observed that while the maritime parts of Carolina were better adapted for commerce and luxury they were not so healthful as the land to the west which was "possessed by wolves, bears, panthers, and other beasts."

Dr. Brickell, a contemporary of Catesby and a physician in the lower Chowan Precinct at Edenton, listed the common diseases as "Agues, or intermittent Fevers, . . . which almost every old Woman pretends to have an infalible Cure for"; cachexia "caused by sedentary habits, green fruits, and eating Clay and Dirt, which the Children, both Whites and Black, and some of the old People are very subject to . . ." corrupting and vitiating the body "through surfeits and ill digestion" which was cured by "strong Purgers, and Exercise . . ." and "Diarrhoea, Dysenteria, Convulsions, Hooping-Cough, Cutaneous Disorders, such as Tetters, Ring-worms, Rashes, prickly-Heats, and the Itch."

Home preparations, based both on traditional wisdom and nonsense, were the chief guardians of the health of the people—and continued to be for the poorer classses through the nineteenth century.

Sassafras was found everywhere and used for almost everything. The tea regulated the bowels; a specific for the gripes was made from the bark of its root; its flower was eaten with salting to cleanse the blood in spring; and its bark was powdered to make a lotion to mundlfy old ulcers and other sores. From the bark of elm root a remedy was prepared for cuts or green wounds and sores; from tulip buds was made an ointment for scalds, inflamations and burns; a tea from dogwood root and bark was a cure for worms; the gum extracted from the sweet-gum in the spring was a cure for herpes and inflamations;

from prickly ash roots was made a preparation for carthartic and an emetic; fermented quince drink was used to purge and cleanse the body; ripe persimmons cleansed wounds and pillitory was used for tooth ache.

Recreation for Rich and Poor

Independent and intemperate habits of the people often led them to violent forms of recreation. While this applied to the country as a whole during the colonial period, in later years the people of Scratch Hall—and to some extent, Sandy Cross—were fabilized for their traditional head-buttings, eye-gougings, slugging and wrestling fests, together with liberal consumption of hard liquors.

In 1754 the Carolina government made it a felony for any person to "unlawfully cut out, or disable the Tongue, put out an Eye, slit the Nose, bite off or cut off a Nose or Lip, bite or cut off or disable any Limb or Member of any subject of his Majesty." Gaming with cards and dice was commonplace.

Dancing was a great diversion among the higher classes. In 1882 Elkanah Watson found a dancing party at the house of a Mr. Granby, a very wealthy planter, near Sunbury. From Brickell it is learned that music was provided by the fiddle and the bagpipe, and in event neither could be procured the people sang for themselves.

The people gathered in great numbers at public meetings, religious meetings, and sports events. In 1712 large crowds turned out to hear Rev. Giles Rainsford preach at one Mr. Garrett's. They were "very ready in their response, as in their method of singing prases to God." Upon a Sunday in 1728 people "from all the adjacent Country" flocked to the quarters of the dividing line commissioners which Byrd supposed was to satisfy their curiosity if their lands would fall in Virginia or Carolina.

At public gatherings one would find the game of "rough

and tumble," "climbing the (soaped and greased) pole," foot race of damsels, chasing greased pigs and other hilarity provoking contests.

Unrestrained Sex Habits

The people of all classes were generally unrestrained in sex habits, which frequently led to fornication and adultery. English men conversed with Indian women who preferred them to less vigorous Indian men; and the presence of white and Negro servants, degraded by their servility, contributed to immorality. It was lamented that Daniel Brett, one of the first Anglican missionaries, was seduced by the sin of fornication.

North Carolina statues, acknowledging sex looseness, placed emphasis on having the parents to care for the children. Isolation of the frontier people made much of their behavior all but unknown to the authorities.

In his "Secret History" Byrd told of five instances where men of the dividing line survey party attempted to impose themselves upon the frontier women. East of the Dismal Swamp at Mr. Merchants,

> "I encampt in his Pasture with the Men, tho' the other Commissioners endug'd themselves so far as to ly in the House. But it seems they broke the Rules of Hospitality, by several gross Freedoms they offer'd to take with our Landlord's Sister. She was indeed a pretty, and therefore it was prudent to send her out of harm's Way."

Two days later,

> "Shoebrush (John Lovick, a Carolina commissioner) & I took a walk into the Woods, and call'd at a Cottage where a Dark Angel surpriz'd us with her Charms. . . . Shoebrush was smitten at the first

Glance, and examined all her neat Proportions with a critical Exactness. She struggled just enough to make her admirer more eager, so that if I had not been there, he wou'd have been in Danger of carrying his Joke a little too far."

Timothy Jones, who accomodated the commissioners with "everything that was necessary . . .

"had a tal straight Daughter of a Yielding Sandy Complexion, who having the curiosity to see the Tent, Puzzlecase (William Little, a Carolina commissioner) gallanted her thither, & might have made her free of it, had not we come reasonably to save the Damsel's Chastity."

West of the Dismal Swamp Peter Brinkley

"had not the good Fortune to please Firebrand (Richard Fitz-William, a Virginia commissioner) with our dinner, But he endeavour'd to mend his Entertainment by making hot Love to honest Ruth, who wou'd by no means be charm'd either with his Perswasion, or his Person. While the Master was employ'd in making Love to one Sister, the man made his passion known to the other, Only he was more boisterous, & employ'd force, when he cou'd not succeed by fair means. Tho' one of the men rescu'd the poor Girl from this violent Lover . . ."

West of the Meherrin River at the plantation of William Kinchen the men drank freely of apple brandy. This made some

"too Choleric, and others too loving. So that a Damsel who came to assist in the Kitchen wou'd certainly have been ravish't, if her timely consent had not prevented the Violence. Nor did my Landlady think herself safe in the hands of such furious Lovers, and therefor fortify'd her Bed chamber & defended it with a Chamber-Pot charg'd to the Brim with Female Ammunition."

While chastity of the frontier woman was constantly in danger, Byrd suggests that some of the women were quite willing to have it threatened.

Class Drinking Habits

The colonial gentleman usually had fine stocks of liquors which he drank at home in moderation, but the lower classes were excessive much as the Indian whom Lawson said was much addicted to drunkeness.

"Their chief liquor is Rum, without any Mixture. . . . They are never contented with a little, but once begun, they must make themselves quite drunk; otherwise they will never rest, but sell all they have in the World, rather than not have their full dose."

By 1715 "the odious and loathsome sin of drunkeness" among the English had "of late grown into common use" and was the "foundation of many sins."

In 1730 Brickell saw crowds of men come into the towns and remain eight or ten days drinking rum, punch and other liquors. Two or three months later they would return for another "Frolick." Gentlemen kept "plenty of Wine, Rum and other Liquors at their own Houses."

Most of the liquors consumed in Scratch Hall, says tradition, were home-made. Persimmon beer from the natural persimmon was greatly esteemed. Apples and peaches produced brandy, and it was said only those men who had sold their souls to the Devil could stomach crab apple brandy. Huckleberries, briarberries and grapes were made into wine. Some of the poorer of the poor gathered poke berries from the hedgerows and made a sort of wine. He who drank it ran the hazard of acquiring a flaming red tongue like old Satan's.

Some women were as addicted to strong drink as the men. Upon the Virginia-Carolina border Byrd observed Thomas Speight and his wife "were so enclin'd to a cheerful Cup, that our Liquor was very unsafe in their keeping. . . . they made themselves happy every day, before the Sun had run one third of his course . . ."

Most of the rum came from New England. It was "so bad and unwholesome," said Byrd, "that it is not improperly call'd 'Kill-Devil.' " It was produced gallon-for-gallon from ropy foreign molasses which was known as "Long Sugar." This molasses also served as a substitute for sugar.

Upon the border sometimes friends were bountifully entertained with a "Capacious Bowl of Bombo," a beverage containing equal parts of rum and water and made palatable with "Long Sugar." The popular beverage was a namesake of Admiral Bombo.

At such time that "good Humor begins to flow" the bowl upon the table was replenished with "Shear Rum" from a "Reserve under the Table."

Such "Generous doings" happened only when "that Balsam of life is in plenty . . ." At other times the Carolinians had not a drop "for their Wives, when they ly in, or are troubled with the Colick or Vapours."

Byrd and his fellow commissioners were supplied with pottle-bottles of strong beer, bottled Maderia wine, and quarts of Jamaica rum.

Horses and Cocks Enchant all Classes

Everyone was enchanted by the horses and cocks — leastwise the gambling which went with the races and the fights—from the stable boy with his half-penny to the gentleman with his extravagant wagers. These were the popular pastimes of the plantations which also drew folks from the flat lands and pine barrens like no other magnet. Tradition tells that race tracks and cock pits were located in most communities, and after the Revolution advertisements and fly bills invited people to travel great distances to these events.

During the colonial period the gentry commonly staged such events with everybody and his ragamuffin brother attending; but early in the ante-bellum period races were held which featured country-style nags. Solomon Ellott of Edenton advertised:

"SPORTING. Will be run for over my Course, on the second Friday and Saturday March 1810, one and two mile heats, free for any nag in Gates, Perquimans and Chowan counties . . . not known as a horse of running fame, or as having won over 100 Dollars in any Race. Two purses, which will be worth sporting for; 1st day 1 mile heats, entrance $10; 2nd day, 2 mile heats, entrance $15." Gate toll was 12½c for a footman, 25c for a horse and 50c for a chair.

In 1787 Elkanah Watson gave a vivid account of a cock fight in nearby Southampton County, Virginia. As he approached the ground in company of a "prominent planter" about 10 o'clock in the morning,

"the scene were alive with carriages, horses, and pedestrians, black and white, hastening to the point of attraction. Several houses formed a spacious square, in the center of which was arranged a large cock-pit; surrounded by many genteel people, promiscuously mingled with the vulgar and debased. Exceedingly beautiful cocks were produced, armed with long, steel-pointed gaffles, which were firmly attached to their natural spurs. The moment the birds were dropped, bets ran high. The little heroes

Cock-Fighting – by Porte Crayon

appeared trained to the business; and were not in the least disconcerted by the crowd or shouting. They stepped about with great apparent pride and dignity; advancing nearer and nearer, they flew upon each other at the same instant, with a rude shock, the gaffles being driven into their bodies and, at times, directly through their heads. Frequently one, or both, would be struck dead at the first blow; but they often fought after being repeatedly pierced, as long as they were able to crawl, and in the agonies of death would often make abortive efforts to raise their heads and strike their antagonists. I soon sickened at this barbarous sport, and retired under the shade of a wide-spread willow, where I was much better entertained, in witnessing a voluntary fight between a wasp and a spider.

"In viewing the crowd, I was greatly astonished to find men of character and intelligence giving their countenance to an amusement so frivolous and scandalous, so abhorrent to every feeling of humanity, and so injurious in its moral influence, by fostering habits of gambling and drinking, in the waste of time, and often in the issues of fighting and duelling."

Cock fighting would remain a popular sport in Gates County through the nineteenth century, but after the Civil War the sport was so frowned upon fights were not held in the open.

Fights were last witnessed about the old plantation areas among descendants of the slaves. As late as 1925 many Negroes raised game chickens on the barnyard for this purpose.

Perkins' Place at Wyanoke on the Chowan River

Houses and Plantations

CHAPTER VII

Crude Pioneer Homes

The first houses between the Chowan River and the Dismal Swamp, according to all available records, were of simple construction. A few may have overlooked the upper Chowan River, where the swamps grudgingly yielded some half-dozen pleasant vistas, and others sat beside Bennetts Creek many miles upstream.

In 1672 George Fox, the Quaker missionary, made mention of a house on Bennetts Creek where "we lay that night by the fireside, the woman lending us a mat to lie on." Thus is implied here was a small frontier home barren of accomodations for visitors.

One of the first homes on the Chowan River seems to have been a shallow cave dug upon the low sandy bluff which overlooks the head of the river from the northeast. About 1688 William Bonner observed "a hole which was in the ground" where the Nottoway and Blackwater rivers merge to form the Chowan and "where one Perkins formerly lived." The home site, now in Gates County, was upon "a piece of Land which Nathan King had kept under an Entry by the name of Wyanoke." Since the bluff rises six to eight feet above the river's surface, the habitation could have been easily made by constructing a simple roof over an excavation in the coarse dry sand.

In 1710, southwest of the Chowan River and opposite the Hall area of Gates County, Virginia and North Carolina commissioners, seeking to resolve the boundary line dispute, spent a night at John Beverly's where they were "lodged in a wretched Kennel of a Loghouse where we could hardly have our length and breadth."

In 1728, when upon the northern border of the Gates County area, William Byrd, a Virginia commissioner for the dividing line survey, observed the houses were of simple construction.

"Most of the Houses in this Part of the country are Log-houses, covered with Pine or Cypress Shingles, 3 feet long, and one broad. They are hung upon Laths with Peggs, and their doors too turn upon Wooden Hinges, and have wooden Locks to Secure them, so that the Building is finished without any Nails or other Iron-Work."

These houses, it seems from the lore of the Hall area, were the better sort to have. They were safer than most others from the intrusion by witches and other unwelcome and mischievious visitors from the spirit realm. While it was known to all that witches customarily shed their skins to pass through the key holes of iron or brass locks, they could enter no door barred by a wooden lock or latch. Until recent years only wooden latches and locks were to be found on the log and slab homes of the area.

The small dwelling was enclosed by a wattle fence, erected to keep out hogs, cows, sheep and other animals. Byrd also explains:

"They also set up their Pales without any Nails at all, and indeed more Securely than those that are Nail'd. There are 3 Rails mortised into the Posts, the lowest of which serves as a Sill with a Groove in the Middle, big enough to receive the End of the Pales: the middle Part of the Pale rests against the Inside of the Next Rail, and the Top of it is brought forward to the outside of the uppermost. Such Wreathing of the Pales in and out makes them stand firm,

[58]

and much harder to unfix than when nail'd in the Ordinary way."

The one or two-room log cabin, with a loft or a "lean-to," enclosed by a paling fence, appears to have been of the better sort of home. Some of the domiciles of the Carolina frontier were quite primitive. "Lean-to" shelters, "log-pen" enclosures half-covered overhead, and hollow-log homes were being used in a make-shift way through the ante-bellum period. Hollows of trees were used for storage purposes up to the twentieth century. At the opening of the eighteenth century Lawson made mention of a tree house.

"I have been informed of a Tulip-Tree, that was ten Foot Diameter; and another wherein a lusty Man had his Bed and Household Furniture, and lived in it till his Labour got him a more fashionable Mansion. He afterwards became a noted Man in this Country for Wealth and Conduct."

The Indian cabin was to be seen in the Hall area when the English began to settle this country. This house was framed round or oval with fire-hardened small poles and then covered over with cypress, juniper or pine bark. The whole was then bound firmly with the bark of the elm tree or grey moss. Upon rare occasions such style houses were used by the English, as was the case of the mariner of Currituck who had obtained the company of a "wanton Female" and of whom Byrd said,

"His Habitation was a Bower, cover'd with Bark after the Indian Fashion, which in that mild Situation protected him pretty well from the Weather. Like the Ravens, he neither plow'd nor sow'd but Subsisted chiefly upon Oysters, which his Handmaid made a Shift to gather from the Adjacent Rocks. Sometimes, too, for Change of Dyet, he sent her to drive up the Neighbour's Cows, to moisten their Mouths with a little Milk.

"But for rainment, he depended mostly upon his length of Beard, and She upon her length of Hair, part of which she brought decently forward, and the rest dangled behind quite down to her Rump, like one of Herodotus's East Indian Pigmies.

"Thus did these Wretches live in a dirty State of Nature, and were mere Adamites, Innocence only excepted."

In one wretched hovel upon the frontier Byrd and his men were "forc't to ly in Bulk upon a very dirty Floor, that was quite alive with Fleas & Chinches," and in another, consisting of "one dirty Room with a dragging Door" that would neither open nor shut, he lodged "very Sociably in the same Apartment with the Family" where nine persons "all pigg'd loveingly together." West of the Roanoke River Byrd found a man

"who liv'd rather in a Penn than a House, with his wife and 6 children . . . The Hovel they lay in had no Roof to cover those wretches from the Injurys of the Weather: but when it rain'd, or was colder than Ordinary, the whole Family took refuge in a Fodder Stack. The poor man had rais'd a kind of a House but for want of Nails it remain'd uncover'd. . . ."

The log house remained a common feature of the Gates County area until after the Revolution when comfortable frame structures became common to the better plantations. The poor people — who were the more numerous — continued to live in small log and slab houses until after the Civil War. After the Revolution the frame houses gradually took preference over the log ones because of the availability of rived pine and cypress boards. These boards—or slabs as they were called—were customarily affixed vertically to the frame of the house, and a second layer was added as crack-breakers. Hand-drawn shingles or slabs covered these and the larger houses.

The slab house was not as tight and warm as the log house. Adrian Parker, Reynoldson Township native, said that it "shed water like a duck, but the fine snows of winter sifted through the cracks."

Hollow trees were used for utility houses in antebellum times, said Old Jack Blount, born on the Abram Parker Place in Hall Township about 1800. He left a story illustrating such utility.

One night while hunting in the Chowan River Pocosin a man grew tired and lay down in the end of a hollow log to take a short nap. Unintentionally he slept until daybreak when he was awakened by a hairy creature anxiously pawing at him. The hunter was startled and ran from his log shelter. Moments later he looked over his shoulder and discovered he was followed by a bear; the bear, by a skunk; and the skunk by a swarm of honey bees. The man then realized the popularity of hollow trees.

The "Hollow Cypress" beside the Barfield Causeway was a traditional roadside shelter soon after the Civil War. When John Crawford was a boy a large opening in its trunk permitted both the fisherman and the traveler to obtain shelter from rain storms. A crude log bench had been installed across one side to provide a rest station.

Crawford recalled how "in olden times" Hall people had driven pegs inside the hollow gum tree and used it for storage. One man "made a good smoke house" of a tree which conducted smoke from an opening in its top. Close by the boat landings hollow logs and trees frequently were used as hiding places for boat paddles and other personal belongings.

Tradition has preserved the name of Mud House Field

Piny Woods Cottage — by Porte Crayon

upon a Chowan River Pocosin ridge north of U. S. 13-158. Noah Felton identifies it as the place where oxen drawing the logwoods "bogey" along rails to Pipkin Landing were quartered. The field had received its name from a house built of mud and poles much like a stack chimney.

Until recent years small log barns, stables, smokehouses and storage houses, constructed of pine and juniper poles, stood near most of the dwellings. A few of these quaint structures still survive in most every community between the Chowan River and the Dismal Swamp.

Large Stack Chimney Common

A large "stack" chimney was common to both the log and frame colonial dwellings, but a few years after the Revolution the better homes were provided the luxury of brick chimneys.

The stack chimney was made by daubing mud about stacked sticks. The interior of the new chimney was made hard by firing. The outside was left for the wind and sun to dry and never became very hard. Erosion by the rain required that the outside be redaubed every few years, with some chimney builders making their rounds three to five years.

The broad chimney base tapered quickly, providing a fireplace well suited for the housewife's cooking chores. Here she broiled or boiled the family's food in pots and skillets and sometimes baked corn pones and sweet potatoes in ashes banked over with live coals. Early in the nineteenth century the village storekeeper in adjacent counties was listing Dutch ovens with his stock of merchandise.

The hearthplace became one of the brighter spots in the lives of both colonial and ante-bellum people. After the evening meal, during the seasons of long nights, the family and occasional neighbors and friends formed the traditional circle before the fire. Imaginations of the children seemingly were set afire by strange stories of the old people and shadows animated by tongues of flame. Here much of the social intimacy of family and friends was born. Here, too, the story tellers, drawing upon English, Indian, and African lore, fashioned the tales to meet the needs of a new country developing from the wilderness.

The Furnishings

The furniture of the frontier home consisted almost entirely of pieces made by father and sons. Usually the bedstead was constructed by laying boards on forked poles attached to joists in the wall. First the straw mattress was used, but gradually this was replaced by more comfortable bedding. At the end of the ante-bellum period the deep feather bed, with the stead hand-made from the heart of the pine and ticking stuffed with downy feathers from the goose or other domestic or wild fowl, was found even in most of the poor homes. The deep warm feather bedding was greatly valued by the dwellers of the "airish" slab houses.

Other furniture apparently was similar to that common to the frontier. The table was made of a split slab supported by legs set in augur holes, and it was matched with three-legged stools made in the same manner. Two small forks attached to a joist held the rifle and shot pouch, and wooden pegs provided a place for hanging clothes and other things.

The home of the pioneer and that of the poor man a century after him was seldom ceiled. As wooden windows and doors were thrown open to let in air and sunshine the industrious woman's floors showed clean, but little she could do about the walls, joists and shingles which had been blackened by wisps of smoke curling from the fireplace and occasional burning of pitch-pine torches and home-made candles.

One could expect to see an iron kettle and frying pan, a few pewter spoons and steel knives brought from the older settlements, and home - made wooden trenchers, bowls, mugs and tubs. From the Indian the Englishman learned that tupelo—"bowl"—gum and sassafras were the woods best suited for making these utensils.

Some of the homes had more elaborate furnishings than ordinary. Clapboard shelves, chests, and extra tables and stools were provided by the father and sons; and feather beds, hand-woven blankets, coverlets, and sheets, gay colored quilts, homespun curtains and tablecloths were products of the industry and artistry of the house-wife and her daughters.

In the unceiled rooms the children, buried snugly beneath the covers, were almost safe from the bugabears, hobgoblins and witches old granny said swarmed through the night sky, as they watched patches of the heavens through holes in the mossy shingle roof.

By the Revolution most of the English had accumulated a few luxury items for both the household and the plantation. Take, for example, the "movable goods" listed in Aaron Harrell's May 14, 1797, will:

"One pot and Skilet, one dish & Bason, one gun, one Froe, one pare Sheep Shears & all my Coopers Tools, one Bed & Jug & six puter Plates, two weeding hoes & one ould ax, one pine chest."

Dorothy Davis, an illiterate woman, provides a sample of the woman's personal belongings in her will of December 30, 1816:

To Barsheba Griffin she willed "one red Cloak, one Bonnett, two Hats, one Petty Coat, 3 Handkerchiefs, one Coppress County Pin;"
To Christen Davis, "one Calico Habit, one Petty

Coat, one Silk Shall, one Bed Quilt, two sheets, one Linen Wheel, one Duch Oven;"
To Dorothy Griffin, "one small Cettle, one frying Pan."

Clearings about most early homes understandably were small, but within a few years, after the slave work force had increased, the young plantations showed marked growth and improvement.

The pioneer Englishman was almost as devoted as the Indian in utilizing the provisions which the country supplied naturally. Thus he customarily left the mulberry, walnut, hicory, chinquapin, chestnut and persimmon in and about his fields. So protected from forest competition, those trees permitted to survive for a number of years attained great size. One celebrated such tree was the old mulberry left in the center of Ballard's Racetrack near Gatesville.

Managers of the better plantations set out orchards of apple trees. These thrived to provide both food and drink. Peach trees and grape vines took somewhat less important places upon the plantations. The hardy scuppernong grape thrived and in time provided harbors of great age.

The gourd in several varieties, the sweet potato hill and the well sweep eventually became familiar scenes at nearly every homeplace. The gourd survived on most soils, and it was found useful for a large assortment of purposes.

The home of the martin—celebrated sentry against the birds of prey—was made by cutting a small door into the side of a gourd. An entire settlement of these homes were provided by hanging so many gourds as desired from the pruned main branches of a small tree or attaching them to cross pieces of an erected pole.

The water dipper was a crook-neck gourd which had one side carved out. The dipper hanged beside the cool spring, at the well or sat in the water bucket—as a cordial host and an ornament to the simple life.

The calendar of the poor Scratch Hall man was made of wooden pegs and gourds. At the beginning of each week seven gourds were hanged to so many pegs, and one gourd was taken down at the end of each day. The custom became so entrenched that each peg came to represent its day of the week.

A small variety of gourd was dried thorougly and used as the baby's rattler. Handy containers for miscellaneous small household necessities were made by carving out gourds of desired sizes.

Traditional Watering Place

The spring path—a narrow well-beaten way leading down the hill through a lush growth of grass, thorns and bushes—was a familiar part of most home sites. Even after the well brought water nearer the home the springside provided greater convenience for washing out the clothes. This patronage was so persistent that the spring became the traditional washing place.

Short sections cut from the hollow cypress and gum trees provided the curbing—the "gums"—for both the spring and the well. Eventually the spring "gums" gathered green moss, and this with a lush growth of vegetation gave the spring a cool and natural atmosphere—whence thoughts of the thirsty turned longingly.

Many of the springs became venerated in lore. Among these were the springs beside the juniper glades from which flowed bitter, "healthful," brandy-colored water. In later years several mineral springs, gushing from hillsides between the great swamps, attracted people from miles about to quaff their health-giving waters and to lay by stocks for home use.

Plantations Reflect Industry

Gates County emerged from the Revolution with some highly developed plantations, as is shown by distribution of slaves and newspaper advertisements.

In 1810 Nathan Creecy was offering for sale his 750 to 800 acre farm which had "a Dwelling House, Kitchen, with Brick Cellar, Barn, Storehouse, Cooper and Blacksmith Shops, with Stables, Negro Quarters, Garden, a good Orchard, a good Well of Water, and everything to compleat a farmer or a merchant. . . ." This land was "best timbered" for white oak and plank pine, lay near a saw mill, and was good range for hogs and cattle.

In 1835 Tillery W. Carr, "desiring to settle in west," advertised his 500-acre plantation on Orapeake Swamp as having 150 acres cleared and "well adopted to cotton." The buildings, erected within the previous ten years at nearly $3,000, consisted of a two-story, forty-foot-long, eight-room house; a 40x30-foot cotton gin house; a cook room and "every other necessary building." The Suffolk to Edenton mail stage passed twice a week. A second tract, containing 148 acres, two miles away was covered with good oak timber.

In 1835 John B. Baker of Coles, near Gates Courthouse, "desirous of moving south," offered "about 1400 acres, large and convenient dwelling, and all the necessary buildings in good repair," a grist and saw mill "usually with 200 barrels of corn a year," a 700 to 800 "Dark Woods" tract producing 1,000 barrels of corn and good crops of cotton.

Industry and Subsistence

CHAPTER VIII

Food in Abundance

Natural and easy to produce foods permitted the first settlers to live without working very hard. To the traditional Carolina diet of "hog and hominy" was added fish, the flesh of beeves, wild animals, wild and domestic fowl, and several kinds of wild fruits and nuts.

While hogs and cattle were found in abundance along the borders of the Dismal and other swamps and pocosins, large quantities of fish and water fowl were available to those people who were convenient to the Chowan River and its tributary creeks. Corn and sweet potatoes could be grown almost anywhere.

In 1709 Rev. William Gordon said that the people of Perquimans and Chowan precincts "feed generally upon salt pork, and some times upon beef, and their bread of Indian corn, which they are forced for want of mills to beat."

William Byrd found the pine barrens upon the Virginia-Carolina border "unfit for Ordinary Tillage" but that they would "bring Cotton and Potatoes in Plenty, and Consequently Food and Rainment to such as are easily contented."

Scratch Hall Fish Lore

In 1713, during the food shortage of the Tuscarora War, Rev. Giles Rainsford wrote from Chowan Precinct that "the whole year is one continued Lent fish being the constant attendant on the Table."

The herring fish, coming from Arctic waters each spring to spawn, was taken in such numbers that it became the chief meat of the poor. Scratch Hall people laid by year-round stores of dried and brined fish; and after the large seine fisheries were established on the Albemarle Sound and its tributary streams late in the eighteenth century, the plantations also supplied themselves with large stocks of preserved fish.

The herring runs were so unfailing that tradition says famine was never known to visit the poor of Scratch Hall. They were considered amply supplied when they had enough fish to serve at breakfast throughout the year and at other meals when fresh meats were in short supply.

Like the Indian, the Hall fisherman built his weirs on the "weak" side of the stream where the water lazed in eddies. The fish hedges were made of white oak splits wattled like the paling fences which surrounder the homes. Smaller splits were laced into oval-shaped fish traps which were anchored upon the bottom of the stream.

The herring was so important to the livelihood of the people that this fish came to represent Scratch Hall frugality, as a fable illustrates:

When an overnight visitor seated himself at the supper table of a Scratch Hall home the landlord normally advised, "Save your (herring) backbone."

Should a puzzled look invite an explanation, the host would add, "You can use it as a candle to go to bed by; and if you are careful not to use it all up, you'll have a comb for your hair tomorrow morning."

The herring abundance provided some of the luxuries of Hall, another fable reveals:

Although the people of old Scratch Hall commonly used the pitch pine torch outdoors, they enjoyed the luxury of the herring candle in their homes.

This candle was made by drying the fish upon hurdles over a slow fire or in the sun. Afterwards the fish was hung up by the head to make the oil of its body settle into its tail. When a person needed a candle the tail was inverted and lighted.

Lazy Men, Industrious Women

John Lawson said that the men of Carolina were "very laborous and make great improvements in their own way." However, he could not give them that character in general." Instead, their easy way of living made them very "neglectful."

Upon the Virginia-Carolina border for the dividing line survey William Byrd said that they were so lazy that, like the Indian, they

"impose all the Work upon the poor Women. They make their Wives rise out of their Beds early in the morning, at the same time that they lye and Snore, till the Sun has run one third of its course, and disperst all the unwholesome Damps. Then, after Stretching and Yawning for half an Hour, they light their Pipes, and, under the Protection of a Cloud of Smoak, venture out into the open Air; tho', if it happens to be never so little cold, they quickly return Shivering into the Chimney corner. When the weather is mild, they stand leaning with both their arms upon the corn-field fence, and gravely consider whether they had best go and take a Small Heat at the Hough: but generally find reason to put it off till another time."

The industrious woman, said Byrd, spun and wove by hand. Cotton, easily produced in the country, was mixed with a little wool for outer garments. The men matched this industry with being "Sloathful in every thing but getting of children . . ."

Little care was spent on the cattle and hogs which rambled the swamps and marshes maintaining themselves through the winter. The hogs grew fat from pine masts which fell in November. Beef and bacon were brined in winter for use during the summer and for export.

The people went without milk and butter during the winter, and in 1752 Bishop Spargenberg observed that "when spring comes the cows are so nearly starved out as to be of little benefit till harvest." Horses had the same fare, and Spargenberg said that perhaps was why they "are not much larger than English Colts—and their cows the size of their yearlings." Hog raising, said Byrd, was managed

"with the least Trouble, and affords the Diet they are most fond of. The Truth of it is the Inhabitants of N Carolina devour so much Swine's flesh, that it fills them full of gross Humors. For want too of a constant Supply of Salt, they are commonly obliged to eat it Fresh, and that begets the highest taint of Scurvy. Thus, whenever a Severe Cold happens to Constitutions thus Vitiated, tis apt to improve into the Yaws, called there very justly the country-Distemper. This has all the Symptoms of the Pox, with this Aggravation, that no Preparation of Mercury will touch it. First it seizes the Throat, next the Palate, and lastly shews its spite to the poore Nose, of which tis apt in a small time treacherously to undermine the Foundation."

In his "Secret History," Byrd accuses North Carolinians with being "extremely hoggish in their Temper, and many of them seem to Grunt rather than Speak in their ordinary conversation."

Game and Fowl for Food

The goose was the most common domestic fowl. She was sufficiently warlike to drive the opossum and mink marauders into their pocosin hideouts; and her shrill cry was a call to her landlord to snatch down his fowling piece.

The deer and bear were generally killed in fall and winter and the surplus meat brined like beef and bacon. Their hunting was regarded as sporting by the English as well as the Indian.

The wild turkey was the largest bird of the forest, and quite numerous. Lawson had seen "about five hundred in a Flock," and he had been told of one weighing nearly sixty pounds. The three kinds which thrived in Gates County fed off acorns, huckleberries and other berries, growing very fat in the fall. Here turkey hunting was a fashionable sport in ante-bellum times. According to local lore,

> The "Moss Head" turkey was the craftiest bird in the forest. He could not be trapped as readily as other types, and he permitted himself to be seen so infrequently that he was regarded much as a phantom. Yet there was one man who proved a match for this wily bird. He was known as "Old Moss Head," so called because of his ability to constantly supply his table with the rare dish. The turkey hunter went to his grave without divulging his secret. Old Jack Blount, plantation story teller, claimed that "Old Moss Head" so perfected his art of turkey calling that when he talked to folks he "gobbled des lak a turkey."

Besides the deer and bear, the poor people hunted the coon, otter, beaver and opossum for both fur and meat. Home-made traps of a large assortment captured these and other animals. Stout log enclosures were built as cow and deer traps, hog traps, and bear traps. The log "dead-fall" was suited for taking the raccoon, mink, polecat, opossum and rabbit. The rabbit "gum" was useful in winter when the rabbit sought to squeeze into a sheltered spot and nibble a bit to eat. Small "dead-falls" and cage traps captured birds, chiefly in winter. Traps set in a planned pattern or series formed a "trap line."

The Legend of Honey Pot

The forest flowers kept the honey bee occupied laying by stores of honey. Watchers of the martin, which followed the homeward flying bee, and the bear found excitement in searching out and robbing the bee tree. Once the tree was found, the bear was said to have shut his eyes, pulled down his ears and set about stealing the honey.

Robbery of a bee tree by an early settler is said to have provided the basis for the Honey Pot legend.

Honey Pot Road crosses Honey Pot Swamp at Honey Pot Bridge three miles east of Gatesville on U. S. 158. The road, swamp and bridge are mentioned in eighteenth century records.

It is said that when the first settlers came to the area the swamp was nameless—until a man found a bee tree in it. The tree was robbed and its honey packed nicely in a pot. The pot, however, was overturned and all the honey spoiled. Afterwards the swamp was known as Honey Pot. When the road and bridge were built they, too, were called Honey Pot.

Fruits of the Forest

Huckleberries of four kinds, growing in the pocosins, ponds and branches and upon the highland, were the most common and abundant wild fruit. They thrived so well in the Hall area that they were woven into the local lore. The woman dried the berries in the sun like the Indian, and the dry berries were stored for making into stews and puddings as desired.

The country also was gifted with the wild grape, gooseberry, strawberry, barberry, mulberry, honey locust, plum, persimmon and paupau apple; the nuts of the hickory, chinquapin, hazelnut and walnut.

The forest also supplied industrious housekeepers with laurel leaves for making of a yellow dye; gallberries and gall of the oak, black dyes; blood root, a red dye; poison vine, a blue-black dye; bar berries, wax for fragrant candles; myrtle berries, a wax for candles with "the most lasting and sweetest smell imaginable;" liveoak acorns, a cocoa substitute and an oil "as sweet as that from the Olive;" and sassafras, a tea.

When Natural Foods Dwindled

By the Revolution much of the forest had been cut away, and wild fruits and animals were not so abundant as they had been. The population also had increased, and most of the people had smaller holdings. With the growing need to conserve food, the Hall woman developed a cookery art which made palatable some foods considered unacceptable to delicate or fashionable stomachs. The meat of animals like the opossum, coon, bear and wild boar and some kinds of fish were first parboiled and treated to remove the offensive flavor or odor and then seasoned and recooked.

Animal fats were used to preserve meats for limited periods, during cool or cold weather. The meat was chopped or ground, formed into paddies and fried until crisp brown. The paddies were dropped into crocks of grease to provide both meat and gravy, as needed, without the cost of salt for brining.

Byrd suggested that some of the pioneer woman's cooking was not appetizing. Beside the Dismal Swamp his landlord's daughter Rachel Speight "regal'd me with a Mess of Hominy toss't up with Rank Butter & Glyster Sugar. This I was forc't to eat, to shew that nothing from so fair a hand cou'd be disagreeable."

The persimmon was the traditional substitute for "Long Sugar" in Scratch Hall. It is said that:

> The host of a Hall home would ask his guest, "How would you like your (sassafras) tea, light or heavy sweet?"
>
> If the answer was, "Light," one persimmon was dropped into the drink; if it was, "Heavy," two persimmons were used.

An occasional home showed the marks of abundance. A few years before the Revolution Smythe found a rare home southwest of the Chowan River which had a table "loaded with fat roasted turkies, geese, and ducks, boiled fowls, large hams, hung beef, barbicued pig, &c. enough for five-and-twenty men."

PART 3

Quaint Storied Gates

CHAPTER IX

New County in Old Area

An act of the North Carolina General Assembly of 1779 took parts of three counties and formed them into Gates. This new county was named for General Horatio Gates who had won the brilliant victory of Saratoga in 1777. After two bloody battles, British General Burgoyne surrendered to him with his entire army.

Before the name of the county was barely known General Gates was dismissed in disgrace. August 15, 1780, as commander of the Southern Revolutionary forces, he was defeated at Camden, South Carolina, with the defeat turning into a rout. However, after Congress had the ex-hero tried for his failure, he was acquitted and restored to his command. By now the war was over and Gates retired. He died April 10, 1806.

Isolation of the country from neighboring courthouses justified establishment of the county, states its charter:

"Whereas by reason of the width of the Chowan River and the difficulty of passing over the same, especially in boisterious weather, it is extremely inconvenient for the inhabitants of the north-east end of the said river, to attend courts and other public business, as also for the convenience of the inhabitants of the north of Chowan and Perquimans Counties, it is necessary that the same be divided into a distinct and separate county."

That part of the new county to the north and west of Bennetts Creek had been in Hertford County since 1759 and that to the south and east of the creek, in Chowan and Perquimans precincts and counties since their formation in 1670.

The seven townships set up were Mintonsville and Folley (later Holly Grove) on the Dismal Swamp; Gatesville, Hasletts and Hunters Mill in the central area; and Hall and Brick House (later Reynoldson) on the Chowan River.

The Hertford area, which had been taken from Chowan earlier, and the Chowan area, says Isaac S. Harrell, usually stood together in politics as opposed to the Perquimans area.

The courthouse was built beside Bennetts Creek on the plantation of James Garrett, and while it was being erected court was held at Kader Riddick's. Some of the first land transfers were recorded in the parent counties and transferred to the new county.

Farm and Forest

The large pocosins, including the Chowan River Swamp and the Great Dismal Swamp, made Gates County predominantly forest country. Even now, about 169,000 of its 219,520 acres are in forests, and one fourth of the forest land lies in the Dismal Swamp.

The plantations were located chiefly in the central area, between numerous smaller swamps and pocosins. These farms, with a few exceptions, were not very large. Where the land was adequately drained they were as productive as those in the more fertile eastern counties.

By the Revolution country stores were serving most of the communities, but as a whole the area looked to the business centers of neighboring Virginia and Carolina counties to handle its forest and farm products. This division apparently discouraged growth of towns, and the natives contented themselves with a quiet and independent way of life. The county, explains Harrell, was influenced little by either the stress of progress or extreme poverty.

Densely Populated

When the first federal census was taken in 1790 the 342-square-mile county was as densely populated and about as prosperous as the other old counties of the east. Of its 5,372 inhabitants 3,080 were free whites, 73 free Negroes, and 2,219 slaves.

There were 348 families who owned slaves and 282 who did not. James Benton of Wiggins Cross Roads, with 40, was the largest slaveholder. Most of the slave holdings were small, with seven families owning more than thirty; 14, twenty-one to thirty; 53, eleven to twenty; 69, six to ten; and 205, five or less. The intimacy provided by the small holdings apparently fostered a mutual feeling of dependence between master and slave. This also encouraged the exchange of ideas and stories and contributed to the development of folk lore.

Quest for Transportation

Inadequate transportation facilities helped to keep the county isolated and prevent the general development of trade. However, this posed no problem as to livestock production, for the animals could be driven overland to the Norfolk market. A flat boat canal, twelve miles across the Dismal Swamp to the George Washington Canal, put the Holly Grove area in touch with Norfolk. Farm and timber products were loaded on barges and poled to market. Bennetts Creek was deep enough to Gatesville to accomodate most boats plying the Chowan River, but it was off the regular commercial route. A few landings upon the Chowan served some of the western settlements.

Ambitious plans for a network of canals after the Revolution never materialized, and it was late in the nineteenth centry before the railroads came. In 1886 Richmond Cedar Works and Roper Lumber Company were at work in the eastern part of the county and a narrow - gauge line was built through Sunbury to Edenton; and in 1887-88 the Norfolk and Carolina Railroad was extended through the western part of the county.

The limited amount of tillable land apparently prevented the county from making much agricultural advancement from 1790 to 1860. The population increased slowly; a few men enlarged their plantations; and forest resources were utilized to a greater extent.

Advancement was retarded by the general depression of the 1830's when new lands were opened up in the south and west. Some of the more industrious farmers—including the Browns, Granberys, Orunds, Carrs and Meamons—left the county.

By 1860, however, the population had increased to 8,442, with increases in all groups. This was comprised of 4,180 free whites, 361 free Negroes, and 3,901 slaves.

Eventually fertility of the land was somewhat improved by drainage and application of composts and fertilizers. Farms were enlarged by taking in new lands, and by 1850 produced were 192,815 bushels of corn, 10,329 bushels of oats, 2,951 bushels of wheat, 1,752 bushels of rye, 86,591 pounds of cotton, and 3,905 pounds of wool. The forests yielded 663 barrels of turpentine and $19,143 worth of lumber while 841 barrels of fish were brined.

As late as 1899 Dr. Thomas M. Riddick spoke of the people as "easy going and quiet, but ever gracious and kindly." It, too, was known that here pride ran so deep a man would not be called a lie, ladies were modest and industrious, and race horses were of the finest stocks.

Evangelists and Camp Meetings

After the Revolution a number of dedicated evangelists introduced Methodism to the county.

Among these was Bishop Asbury who made several visits to the area between 1782 and 1810. In 1785 he stopped at "brother Redrick's . . . where I spoke a little." Three years later he preached six miles north of Gatesville at Knotty Pine where there was an Episcopal chapel, but with few people attending "it was a barren meeting." A man named Newby, who was a Quaker, "entertained us kindly," and Asbury arrived at "sister Gipson's, cold and weary.

In 1791 Asbury saw "Sister (Judith) Baker" at Knotty Pine, and at Gates Courthouse he was heard by "many serious people." From hence he rode to Constant's Chapel, an Anglican church "on one of the branches of Bennett's Creek" at Sunbury. He stayed with Isaac Hunter and had "a happy meeting with the poor Africans at night."

Returning from a visit to the county in 1801 Asbury crossed over the Chowan River at Winton. On the northeast approach he was "benighted in the swamp, which for two miles was overflowed with water." In 1804 he spoke at the courthouse and that night at the house of Daniel Southall, a Methodist preacher. Back at Southall's in 1906 he was "pleased to see so many come out upon so short notice." Asbury's last recorded trip was January 1810 with the weather "pleasant but cold, cold!"

March 17, 1799, Mrs. Baker of Knotty Pine Chapel wrote Asbury a letter reporting on those of the flock who had passed away. For example:

"Ann Gipson, converted from the height of pride and vanity to a humble lover of God and man; full of good works.

"Mary Hays, a dear, simple, humble, tender affectionate woman.

"Mary Parker, who had much forgiven, and loved much.

"Milberry Billips, a tender-hearted, loving woman, her husband a gross backslider; he brought his family to poverty; she died a few days after her husband, of a broken heart, as was supposed. Oh, the few happy matches!"

A camp meeting—with Phillip Bruce, presiding elder, and Enoch Jones, assistant—was announced to be held within a mile of Gates Courthouse beginning June 10, 1808. Visitors were asked to "come provided with tents and other necessary provisions, to continue on the ground during the full period." Those arriving by water at Bennetts Creek Bridge would be "furnished with land carriage from the Bridge to the Camp ground." Those coming without their own accomodations "will be furnished at the Court House on reasonable terms."

The traditional camp ground site is on U. S. 158A northwest of Gatesville.

William D. Valentine, Winton diarist, provides a view of one of the humble Methodist evangelists in 1842:

"Just now a mean looking horse and vehicle attracted attention along the streets (of Winton). The covered waggon was shackly and the horse poor, but the man in the covered cart is one of the most eminent divines of the Methodist church in this section of N. Carolina and Virginia. It is the Rev. Ethelbert Drake. . . ."

The first Methodist church was established at Savages in 1811, and Parkers was built in 1813. Tradition says this church was an outgrowth of a society organized by Asbury about 1800.

The Baptist movement developed chiefly by division of memberships. In 1806 Middle Swamp Baptist Church was established by separation from Meherrin at Murfreesboro.

Damascus was the first Christian church, opening in 1832, and it remained alone in the field until after the Civil War.

Before 1860 there were four Baptist, eight Methodist, and one Christian churches. All the Episcopal chapels had been abandoned soon after the Revolution.

Eureka Baptist congregation got their church going in 1878 while meeting under a bush harbor. Dr. R. E. Parker gave the land for a church building, but a few years later when the doctor was asked for more land for a cemetery, he is quoted as having said: "I gave you the land to save them. But you'll have to find a place to get clear of them."

Early Schools

Mr. Marshburn's school at Sarem in 1712 was one of the first mentioned in North Carolina. Tradition remembers this as an Indian school while Rev. Giles Rainsford said it was open to both English and Indian students.

Spring Hill Academy was established in 1820, and several academies followed—at Reynoldson, Buckland, Gatesville and Sunbury.

The public school system began in 1840 with five common schools spread over the county. Ten years later there were twelve one-teacher schools.

The Free Negro

Although the free Negro had come into Gates County during the colonial period, he was not sufficiently numerous to cause much apprehension until the 1831 Southampton County, Virginia, massacre. There, however, was an increase from 111 to 327 between 1810 and 1830. This is credited to some white masters taking slave concbines and immigration from Virginia. In 1844 fourteen free Negroes bearing names of Collins, Boon, Brown and Copleand were indicted by the grand jury for coming from Virginia without permission.

The recession of the 1830's and strict state laws against free movement of the Negro apparently caused northward migration. During this period the number of slaves increased slightly and the free Negroes decreased some.

In 1850 all the free Negroes were listed as having white blood, and white parentage is further supported by the fact that more than one half of the men could read and write.

New Hope Baptist Church was built in 1859 for free Negroes, and tradition states that it was a long time after the Civil War before a "shot-free" Negro would be accepted into membership.

As a rule the free Negro and the poor white man lived on lands little suited to agriculture, and this included the wet flat lands, the sandy pine ridges, and remote necks of land. Tradition states that the land-hungry poor often consoled their grievances against the landed rich with the saying, "The bottom rail always comes to the top." Then, after the Civil War, as some plantations fell to pieces, they cited the wisdom of the old saying.

The free Negro, made alert by necessity, usually developed special skills to gain employment. It also fell his lot to perform both seasonal tasks and those too hazardous for use of valuable slaves. He found work at the seine fisheries, produced tar and turpentine, and made shingles and staves.

The Fisherman's Court

Hiring of hands for the fisheries on the Albemarle Sound and Chowan River caused the February court at

Gatesville—as at all other county seats of counties along the Chowan—to be known as Fisherman's Court, which in Gates was also called "Hiring Day."

The herring and shad fishermen came to this court to hire men—usually free Negroes—for the spring season, and men came to be hired.

In 1841 William D. Valentine stated that one such court at nearby Winton was attended by

"not less than a thousand people composed of fishermen, suitors, and businessmen—free negroes, gentlemen, loafers, mulatto girls, stud horses, men of fine clothes and whiskers, lawyers, doctors and the duce knows what not . . . fishermen go there to hire hands, and the hirelings go to be hired."

Laying by of year-long stores of herrings was customary until recent years, as is observed by an April 30, 1897, newspaper note. Fish carts were passing through Gatesville "constantly on their way to the lower fisheries." The attraction—herrings were selling for fifty cents per thousand!

Lenient Masters

The master was generally kind to the slave, with the slave being considered both as a dependent and valuable property. Along the Dismal Swamp the small slaveholder is said to have shut his eyes while his slaves aided escaped slaves to find sanctuary.

Isaac S. Harrell tells of Gilbert Copeland, a slave who in 1843 was hired out by his master to one Parker. The day before the slave was to be returned Parker sought to punish him. Gilbert ran and Parker shot him in the back at ten feet, with only the smallness of the shot saving his life. The State Supreme Court upheld a ruling by the lower court that since the slave had shown no resistance

[85]

his master should be compensated.

Frequently the master was proud of the slave who became skilled in his work or distinguished himself in the manly sports of fighting, wrestling, running and hunting. The slave was entered into competition with other slaves at public events.

Although patrolers were appointed in all districts after passage of the 1833 State patrol act, there was no noticeable change in slave relations. Masters readily gave trusty slaves written authority to move about freely.

A Sunbury man, says Miss Lucy Costen, gave one of his servants a note which read, "Don't hurt my nigger."

Old Jack Blount left stories of the traditional master-servant relationship and envy of the poor whites for the well cared for and pampered slaves.

Fleet-Footed Carter Brothers

A close friendship grew between Jim Carter of Hall Township and his two slaves, brothers Sam and Jerry. They were about the same age and received the care of the slave boys' black mammy, nursing them all alike.

As surely as had been forecast, they were to listen to Old Mammy's stories and fish and hunt together. Thus when Sam and Jerry became Jim's slaves by inheritance their friendship did not waver.

Jerry acquired his first mark of distinction when venerated Old Black 'Lijah of the Carter plantation, bowed by his infirmities, selected the slave youth to carry on with his conjure wisdom. This in later years won Jerry notoriety as a wart remover.

As young men—when Jim Carter's plantation was full of youthful frolic —Sam and Jerry won distinction for their racing achievements.

Carter was known as one of those lenient masters who didn't hear, or pretended not to hear, his servants, when they assembled in the kitchen and danced far into the night. Although some masters were indicted for permitting their slaves to assemble unlawfully no charges seem to have been brought against Carter.

Jerry won the Gates County foot-racing championship at a fair in Gatesville, and Jim Carter was said to have made some large winnings.

Jerry virtually bursted his buttons with pride for some time, and young John Brantley, the newly appointed patroler for the Hall area, warned him he best not be caught off the Carter plantation without a permit—"You'll find your feet won't take you as fast as you might want to go!"

News of the patroler's threat quickly got around, but people interpreted it to be more of a challenge to Jerry's racing skill than a restraint to his freedom. Soon it was learned that Jim Carter had agreed to let his slave foot-race the mounted patroler. But to even the odds Jerry was to be permitted to choose the course.

A time was chosen which permitted everyone who wished to attend, and this included masters and slaves from the neighboring plantations, poor whites from the sand ridges and free Negroes from the flat lands. And on the appointed day people turned out as if it had been a horse race or cock fight. They partook of their usual frolic—picnicked, drank brandy and laid down their bets.

Jerry was given three hundred paces from the starting point he had chosen. Brantley whipped his horse and quickly gained ground, but the footman darted from the public road down a hedgerow. From there on it was over fences, through thickets, and across the mill pond on a waiting skiff.

Jerry's course required long detours by his adversary, and he had been sitting out front of his cabin waiting several minutes when Brantley rode up.

The patroler was greeted with, "Where has you been all dis time, 'Boss!'"

Jerry's brother Sam was called "Fox," because Jim Carter frequently carried him fox hunting.

On these ocassions Sam did not ride with his master. He, instead, helped the dogs with the chase. It was his job to run from thicket to thicket ahead of the fox and to frighten him on through. In this way the fox was unable to "fox around" and confuse the dogs.

Marster "Cracklin' Jack" Parker

In the late ante-bellum period western Gates County had two Jack Parkers, and folks distinguished them after their own likes, which was to the dislike of both.

The scrawny patroler of Hall Township was called "Cracklin' Jack" Parker, and the large muscular fellow of the Bear Garden area near Sarem in Reynoldson Township, "Bear Garden Jack" Parker.

Eventually Jim Carter's fast-running slave Jerry was caught out of bounds without a permit. His plea that he had gone three miles to the Story place to learn of the blacksmith how to make an iron wedge did not save him from the prescribed whipping.

However, Jerry was offered his choice of patrolers to administer the whipping. He promptly replied, "I'll take Marster 'Cracklin' Jack,' " who was his neighbor in Hall.

Jerry unwittingly made a good choice bad by calling this Jack by his detested nickname.

The patroler poured on the maximum number of lashes as barked by his companion while Jerry's cries mounted, "Don't hit so hard, Marster 'Cracklin' Jack!' "

Dr. Bob Ballard, Fabled Slaveholder

Although a few men eventually acquired large numbers of slaves, after the Revolution the distribution among the people generally remained little changed. In 1860 Mills

Roberts of Mintonsville Township had as many as one hundred; a half dozen men owned as many as seventy-five; and twenty held as many as fifty.

Dr. Bob Ballard of Hall Township was regarded as one of the more successful large slave holders. He was an enterprising farmer and a good business man, remembered in local lore as a man of great wealth and many peculiarities.

It was said that once he had so many slaves he did not know them all. Since he operated a grist mill and a saw mill at Ballard's Pond (earlier Parker's Pond and later Taylor's Pond), there were frequent goings and comings of both whites and blacks. One day he asked a black man, "Whose nigger is you?"

"I'se Marse Ballard's," Marse Ballard was told.

Ballard had the reputation of being kind to his slaves; but it was added that his wife was largely responsible, for she would not permit him to have them whipped.

A part of his fortune was built on raising Negroes for sale, and he usually offered them on the Richmond, Virginia, market. He received gold for them and brought it home and hoarded in an ancient brass banded trunk. Those who chanced to see it said it was similar to the old trunks described in pirate lore.

Ballard was as hard on the poor as he was lenient with his "niggers." This may have been because these whites represented the economic inequity which had developed chiefly after the Revolution and that they were suspected of readily receiving goods which had been stolen from him by his slaves.

Mulatto children born to two white spinsters were said to have been fathered by two of his slaves who thieved in their behalf.

Ballard held the poor whites in so great contempt it was said that when one came to his home he was required to go to the back door the same as the Negro servants.

Once when a poor fellow from Ellis Ridge asked, "Mr. Ballard, give me a chaw uv terbakker," he was instructed to say, Please!"

"Please!" the fellow readily begged.

"Come and get it," Ballard retorted as he cut off a piece and threw it upon the floor.

Ballard loved to sport—fox hunt, fish and race horses. Races on the old mile-long track across his plantation were held at regular intervals. Racing was made a homey event during his time. Basket lunches were brought and picnics were spread. Brandy and other liquors were passed about freely.

An extravagant tale was told about a large cake prepared for one of the races. It was decided to make just one "pudding" cake instead of several small ones. The flour, sugar, eggs and shortning were brought to the scene and there prepared. The men fetched small forked trees from the woods and built a hurdle over a large log heap. However, while the cake was cooking the supports gave way, and a score of Hall men died in the steaming mixture.

Ballard was recognized for his improved farming methods. He used better plows and manures to restore the over worn lands of his forefathers, and he made large areas of fertile low lands usable by cutting canals and ditches.

Rice Patch and Pole Creek

Local lore points to Ballard's rice growing success under difficult circumstances as evidence of his ingenuity. He supplied the rice needs of his plantation and had large quantities to sell.

One of his fields was a 30-acre tract, still known as the Rice Patch, beside old Gatesville Ferry Road two miles west of Gatesville. He sent his slaves into Troy

Swamp, cleared back the marsh, cut a canal to Bennetts Creek and threw up a dike.

J. D. Baines quotes Old Tom Willey, who worked in the Rice Patch for Ballard, as having said the canal utilized the rare wind-controlled tides of the Chowan River to regulate the water level in the field. The canal received the name Pole Creek because dugout canoes laden with rice were poled to Bennetts Creek where larger boats received their cargoes.

The Brandy Tree

When the old race track at Ballard's was laid out respect for the wild mulberry was so great that one of the stately trees was allowed to remain in the middle of the way. The track graciously parted and passed to either side of it.

Eventually the public road between the new Court House at present Gatesville and Eure and the racetrack became as one for that mile. Maintenance became the responsibility of the district road crews which kept the holes filled and the bushes cut back.

At that time it was customary to dram the workmen of the spade and shovel detail. Thus the overseer brought along an adequate supply of apple brandy.

One day the quart bottle of brandy was put into the hollow of the old mulberry for temporary safe-keeping. The hole was deeper than contemplated, and the bottle fell beyond arm's reach of all the thirsty men. Some wanted to cut into the tree after it, but the mulberry was saved by fetching of another bottle of brandy.

Although it became common knowledge that the tree stubbornly hoarded a quart of the county's best elixir, no person dared molest it. Yet long-armed persons of each generation—gathering for the races or traveling the hot dusty way—made it something of a contest to probe for the rare prize. All were disappointed, until the state's road building program decreed that the tree should come down.

It was a prohibition-period road gang which dug into the rotten debris of the felled brandy tree's stump and summoned into the light the sparkling container of traditional "happiness."

The Moccasin Cypress

A large hollow cypress tree in the mash beside Williams' Mill Pond upon the upper course of Bennetts Creek was pointed to as the Moccasin Cypress, and with it went a tale as related by an ancient miller.

One day this miller discovered several snakes stretched out side by side dead near the tree, and a few days later there were several more at the same spot.

As time crept on the phenomena was repeated in an orderly mysterious pattern.

The miller, who was said to have kept a curious eye ever alert to visitation of witches to his dusty cobweb draped mill house, began to cast habitual glances across the nearby marsh to learn of the uncommon goings on there.

One day he dropped his tasks to watch as his interest was attracted by a king snake. The snake went to each clump of grass and every fallen tree and tree stump. Water moccasins lying there ran for safety into the hollow of the cypress tree.

When the king snake had completed his rounds he took up guard near the tree. There he waited out the hours, and as the moccasins sought to escape he caught them one by one and choked them to death.

The king snake remained unmolested for several years, and his death trap came to be known as the Moccasin Cypress.

The Impossible Thief

Thieving was one of the more common complaints against the slave, and at times the customary whipping of offenders seemed to avail the masters little.

One little Negro slave of Sunbury, says Miss Lucy Costen, won notoriety for his dedication to thievery.

"You've got to break that pickaninny from stealing," the boy's mother was told by her master. She tried the customary deterrents—from whipping to hard tasking—but none seemed to do any good.

One day, in desperation, she tied her son upside down to a tree. That didn't work either, for people were horrified by the cruelty and made her untie him.

Finally, she conceived of a fright cure. She filled the boy with ghost stories and tied him to a headstone in haunted Damascus Church graveyard.

"Lawdy mercy!" she threw up her hands in desperation and cried as she learned of the results.

The little thief had stolen the flowers from the grave!

General Joseph Riddick

General Josheph Riddick, one of Gates County's leading citizens from the American Revolution until his death in 1839, is representative of the humble and practical character of the people.

Riddick seldom left his plantation near Sandy Point Baptist Church beside the Dismal Swamp except in his stick gig. Although he could have afforded a train of elaborate carriages, he preferred the two-wheeled gig, the carriage of the middle classes. Riddick found it the best vehicle for the bad roads of his time, it being so light that a horse could draw it with ease through all but the worst of the quagmires.

Riddick served in the House of Commons 1771-1774; for twenty-five years was a member of the State Senate, as its speaker 1800-1804 and 1806-1811; and served additional terms as member of the upper house 1815 and 1817. This thirty-term record in the assembly has never been challenged by another North Carolinian.

Tradition states that General Riddick always made the trip from Gates County to Raleigh in his stick gig and put up at the Locust Tavern at the corner of Raleigh and Hillsboro streets. His gig never failed him over the worst roads. Usually he arrived in Raleigh on time and never missed a session.

Wedding Match Broken Up

Traditional stories state that courting men from neighboring communities and distant parts were made unwelcome in some sections of Gates County. Local young men, according to their ability and temper, had their particular method of handling the suitors.

Fort Islanders were said to have formed gangs, waylaid and engaged the unwanted suitor in physical combat; and thus many a young woman was seen safely wed in her community.

James Figures, according to the March 17, 1814, Murfreesboro "Hornet's Nest," fell into a "hornet's nest" as he went seeking a Gates County bride. The poor fellow was victimized by "ramscamptious conduct."

The Monday preceding he had gone "in the full expectation of bringing home a wife." He, instead, was "greatly disappointed by the unjustifiable, abominable, notorious, rumbunctious and scampacious conduct of one Wm. Wiggins" whom he credited with breaking up the match.

The reason, Figures asserted, was that Wiggins "could not get the girl himself."

Wiggins and his sister Rebecca "told as many lies on me as they could well make out to be true, all of which I am able to prove false by as good men or better than are in the county."

Figures had been led to believe that Wiggins enlisted the assistance of his brother-in-law, William Wiggins, who went to the girl's house "just before" the suitor's arrival. The consideration was said to have been fifty dollars which William had better kept "to pay some of his debts."

Figures was "almost fumigated with wrath, but on reflection recomposed myself and returned home in as high spirits as ever I was in all my life." While the shock was "monstratiously great" it "did not destroy my appetite for as good a dinner as ever was prepared on such an occasion; and which I partook of on my return."

Figures could not refrain from exposing such "rampscamptious conduct" of the plotters and "execrating my own conduct in the affair which has been uniformly honourable and upright as become a gentleman and a man of honor."

One Eyed Horses and a Rare Character

D. H. Strother, roving correspondent for Harper's Magazine as Porte Crayon, made some off-beat representations of Gates County in the March 1857 issue.

Upon the steamer Stag, journeying down the Chowan, an absurd and exaggerated story was represented by a passenger as "a Gatesville story."

A close-up view of a Gates County native was had at Belvidere Fishery on the Albemarle Sound near Edenton as a train of carts came down for annual fish stores.

Strother seemingly had been acquainted with the fable which represented Scratch Hall people as being one-membered. He professed to be struck by

"a train of Gates County buggies, conducted by natives from the interior, come to buy fish.

"The buggy, so called probably in derision, is a

A Native — by Porte Crayon

cart covered with a white cotton awning, drawn by a bony, barefooted horse with one eye. This is not a Cyclopean monster, as one versed in the classics might imagine, for the eye is not located in the middle of the forehead, but on the side, and the animal, on an average, is rather below the medium size. Nor were we able to ascertain whether Gates County furnished a one-eyed breed of horses, for our visitors from the interior are not communicative, their silence being apparently the result of diffidence. But they are acute observers, and as sharp as a mowing-scythe at a bargain.

"That chap with the sorrell head would make a rare sketch.'

" 'Neighbor,' said the manager (of the fishery), if you will sit for your portrait to this gentleman I'll make you a present of that fine string of rock-fish.'

"The native paused and looked at Crayon, who was busy pointing his pencils.

" 'I don't see, said he, tartly, 'that I am any uglier than the rest of 'em.'

" 'Certainly not, my friend,' said Crayon, 'you misapprehend my motive entirely. I merely desired your portrait as a remembrance, or rather a specimen—or a—' Here our artist closed up, and the manager snickered outright.

" 'I'll tell you what, Mister, you needn't think to make a fool of me; if you'll jest take a lookin' glass, and picter off what you see in it, you'll have a very good specimen of a bar.'

" 'But, neighbor, don't go off at half-cock; here's another superb rock I'll add to the bunch.'

"The indignant countryman hesitated, and weighed the fish in his hand. 'Well, you may take me if you can catch me while I'm bobbin' around, but I can't stop for you.' "

Major Bulbous — by Porte Crayon

[98]

Major Bulbous

Strother told the ludicrous story of one Major Bulbous, a character apparently residing somewhere east of the Chowan River, and his stick gig after a relation given by a stage coach driver. The coachman had once seen the fabled Major in his gig

" 'atwix G(atesville) and E(denton), where I druv a coach for a while, a-coming up through the Piny Woods, in sich a pickle as I never see a man before or sence. At fust I thought it was one of these steam-engines tearing along the road by itself, but as he come alongside I see it was the Major in his gig. His skin was pretty full, he was driving like thunder, and his gig all afire. "Hallo, Major," says I, "stop!" But he only cussed me black and blue. Then one of the passengers cried out, "Hallo, old fellow, whar did you come from?" "From hell," says he, giving his hoss the whip. "Well, I should have thought so from appearances," said the passenger. By this time the Major was out of sight, leaving a streak of smoke behind him, perhaps a quarter of a mile long. No doubt the gig caught fire from a cigar, for he was much in the habit of smoking as he traveled."

"And what became of him?"

" 'Why, they say, in passing through the swamp near his house, the wheel struck a cypress-knee and flung him out into the water. The horse run home with the gig in a blaze, and made straight for the barn-yard. By good luck the gate was shut, or he might have set the whole premises on fire. They say the Major didn't get drunk for well nigh a month afterward.' "

The First Rail Coach

Although it was long after the Civil War before the first railroad reached Gates County, the first coach used on the Portsmouth and Weldon Railroad was said to have been built at Buckland in the 1830's.

But when the coach had been completed it had to be transported to the rail line. This was done by mounting the car on skids and drawing it on greased poles some twenty miles along the country roads to Blackwater Depot near present Franklin, Virginia.

Smart Heads Humbugged

May 1842 a phrenologist "examined the heads of many persons at Bertie, Hertford, and Gates," told of persons' characters and "made much money." All did not fall for his humbuggery, chuckled William D. Valentine.

Stumper Makes Dry Haul

Until not so many years ago a liberal supply of apple brandy was the best vote getter of all, and after the drinking got under way it was not too objectionable for a stumper to state his case.

However, at Jonesville (Corapeake) on the western rim of the Dismal Swamp, precedent was broken on one occasion. A stumper opposed to Grover Cleveland brought along a keg of brandy complete with a gourd dipper and set up on John Jones' lawn. The audience paid lots of attention to the brandy but little to the speaker. His day was completely lost, says Horace Barnes, when a bear came ambling across a field and men and dogs went after him.

The election, too, was lost. Cleveland carried the county.

Fabled Scratch Hall

CHAPTER X

Fabled Forest Country

The forest wilds of Scratch Hall provided a last sanctuary for the North Carolina myth, as the state turned progressive and began to rout the long perpetuated stories of its backwardness.

The Chowan River and its pocosins erected a barrier so formidable that few of the natives seldom left Scratch Hall and rarely did an outsider wander from the main ways while traversing the fabled country.

The forest dwellers were not very helpful in dispelling the mystery. They had clung so tenaciously to the habits and customs of their foreparents that by the Civil War they were regarded as clannish and not very communicative with people outside their own group.

Thus two Halls were created—the realistic Hall as known by the natives and the fabilized Scratch Hall oasis as depicted from without.

In 1828 Captain Basil H. Hall, an officer in the British Royal Navy, was struck by the wild and mysterious appearance of the Scratch Hall country as he journeyed through it enroute from Norfolk, Virginia, into North Carolina.

It being in February and with intercolonial travel "almost as periodical as the season," the Captain and Mrs. Hall had the three-times-weekly mail stage almost to themselves.

The first stop in Carolina was at Winton to the west of the Chowan River. Early nightfall of the short winter

Piny Woods — by Porte Crayon

day made it necessary for the last part of the journey, that through the Scratch Hall pine barrens and pocosins, be made at night. Of this Hall said,

". . . The road for about twelve miles passed through a dense forest of pines and junipers rising out of a continued swamp, along which the carriage way seemed to be floated on poles, or trunks of small trees, laid across; which being covered with nothing but a thin stratum of earth and leaves, was fearfully jolty. The evening, moreover, was so dark, that the forest on each side of us stood up to the height of sixty feet like a perpendicular cliff of coal, with a narrow belt of sky above, serving no other purpose than to point out the way, by a feeble ghost-like reflection upon the ditches on either side, which looked as if they were filled with ink.

"It was a sort of guesswork driving; for we came every now and then to pools a quarter of a mile in length, through which the horses splashed and floundered along, as well as they might, drawing the carriage after them in spite of the holes, into which the fore-wheels were dipped almost to the axletrees, making every part of the vehicle creak again. These sounds were echoed back with a melancholy tone from the desolate blank on both sides, mingled with the croaking of a million frogs, whose clear, sharp note, however, gave some relaxation to the ear from the gloomy silence of this most dreary of forests.

"Anything was a relief after the amphibious sort of navigation through such a tunnel as this, and we breathed more freely on reaching the banks of the river Chowan . . . We were ferried across the stream by slaves who stuck several torches made of the pitch-pine tree, into the sides of the scow, or flat.

This blaze of light immediately about us made the solitude and silence of the forest in our rear even more impressive than it had appeared, when we ourselves were almost lost in gloom.".

In 1861 a correspondent to the "New York Tribune" found that the road through Scratch Hall from Winton to Gatesville "is mostly over sand hills, your horse wading through silicious dust about a foot deep" and that night travel was prevalent in hot weather. The last three or four miles next to Winton "lay through a swamp, the water of an amber hue, and averaging two feet in depth."

A short while afterwards a Confederate purchasing agent stated that the swamp lands were "overgrown with cypress and juniper trees, with a heavy undergrowth of reeds," and beyond these lay the sandy lands covered with large pines which had been made famous as a tar-making region. In these swamps and pine forests, it was added, lived "a number of very ignorant and miserably poor people." Their traditional Scratch Hall country extended seven miles from the Chowan River opposite Winton along the road to Gatesville.

In February 1860 a correspondent of the "Southern Argus" of Norfolk, Virginia, enroute to Winton, was captured by evening shadows stalking from unfriendly swamps onto the Chowan River causeway.

All at once his mare began to "tremble like an aspen leaf," and looking about he saw "a bear moving slowly toward us." Unfortunately unarmed, he struck the rowels in his steed and "dashed by the ugly customer" and on towards the river with the horse breaking the thin ice with every leap.

The swampy brink of the river was without habitation, and flitting clouds pranked, occasionally covered up the moon. He received no answer to his cries for help, only his own echoes bounding back from the swamp. After an

[104]

anxious half-hour, a crew across the river, noisily loading a schooner with staves, heard him and sent across the ferryman "much to my joy."

Homes Hidden Away

Although the much-traveled intercolonial roads cut narrow openings through the forests of Hall, the wildness of the country commenced at the very roadsides and extended in all directions. Few habitations were on the main ways and the inhabitants encountered were not communicative. For the most part, the people chose to hide their simple cabins in the mysterious recesses of the woodlands, and these were served chiefly by footpaths. The occasional cart trail was overgrown and little traveled. The stranger dared not leave the main way for fear he might become lost or meet with some uncertain fate. Traditon long has conveyed the belief that the wilds stood as a defense against civil authority and that the man who intruded upon this region with unannounced business was regarded with grave suspicion.

It was the swamp and pocosin barriers which made foot travel the more convenient mode. Footways spread over the area much like a spider's web, along the ridges and across branches, pocosins and swamps — providing the "short cuts." A few hundred yards by one of these paths to a neighbor's house beyond the branch, spanned by a "footbridge," often would save many miles around by road. It served the same purpose as the over-the-ridge trail to the next hollow in the mountains.

A footbridge in Hall meant anything from a pole thrown across a wet place in the path to thick planks or logs laid on cypress blocks and pegged or nailed securely. Sometimes hand railings were made by laying poles in the forks of inverted sections of small trees driven into the earth. However, these were considered a luxury of

Hacking the Pine, Hauling Resin to Market, and Cottage

[106]

the intercolonial ways. They were needed little on the by-ways used by the surefooted natives.

"Scratch Hall" Origin Fables

No one seems to know for certain how Scratch Hall obtained its name, although both its inhabitants and their neighbors have eagerly sought to pierce the mystery a good many years.

The most that has been turned up are a few records which reveal the name pre-dates Hall Township and that there was a branch and a pocosin by the name in the early eighteenth century.

The imagination, on the other hand, has been permitted free exercise, and there are several fables which explain the name's origin. In one of these some natives say:

> In that remote time when the Scratch Hall sect-ion was known merely as the pocosins and sand ridges east of the Chowan River its inhabitants were so poor that they did not have money with which to buy buttons for their homemade clothes. Thus it grew customary as each fall brought the threat of cold weather for them to sew themselves snugly into their woolen underwear. When spring came with its warm sun "all" came from their woolen cocoons and "all" were ready for an enthusiastic scratch. Scratch-ing went on in "all" parts of the woods and over "all" parts of the body. The scratching phenomena was so widespread that people of neighboring areas called the scratchers "Scratch-alls" and their locality "Scratch - all." Later on the sound was changed slightly and the name became more dignified as "Scratch Hall."

One group of story tellers agree the name originally was "Scratch-all," but they contend this was because all of its women would scratch and all of its men, fight.

Still others, among them Hall natives, state the name was a gift of a group of fighting and scratching Indians. The listener is asked to believe:

When the English began to erect their first cabins in the Scratch Hall area they had as their neighbors a tribe of Indians who had swapped names like Hungry Bear, Balhead Eagle, and Wise Old Owl for the paleface's Hall. Just why they liked Hall remains unknown; but it is suggested that it may have been tossed in by the English traders as good measure with their rot-gut rum. As soon as the Indians had latched onto the name and the brew "all hell" broke loose. Then, visit after visit, the fur-laden traders retired to civilization leaving the Halls fighting and scratching among themselves. Eventually the Hall Indians became known as the "Scratching Halls," a branch supplying them with water, "Scratch Hall Branch," and their cluster of bark-covered homes, "Scratch Hall."

A few Hall natives offer a practical explanation and claim the wildness of their country accounted for its name. They have learned from tradition:

Most of Hall Township was thickly wooded until late in the nineteenth century. Trees of the virgin forest, both of the pocosins and the sand ridges, sought to out-tower each other while they drew their foilage as an endless curtain against the sky. The first dark ways, blazed by the Indian and beaten by the Englishman, disturbed the forest very little. Not a single tree giant was felled by fire or axe, and the pathways wound through the shadows quite like endless halls. The "Scratch" was added years later when the poor people of the sand ridges began to "scratch" for a living.

The name "Scratch Hall" was well established early in the eighteenth century. On June 4, 1728, three months after the Virginia-Carolina dividing line survey made it known the area lay in North Carolina, John Nairn and his wife Mary sold 200 acres "on West Side of Scratch Hall Pocosin" to Wm. Umfleet of Nansemond County, Virginia.

Land of Tar, Pitch and Turpentine

Soon after the Tuscarora War of 1712-13 a wave of settlers, chiefly from Virginia, took out land grants upon the pine barrens of western Gates County.

They obtained, in addition to good livestock grazing land, resources for development of forest industries. The sand ridges provided the pine forests for production of naval stores; the hard-bottom pocosins, oak trees for stave making; and the soft-bottom pocosins, juniper and cypress forests for shingle production. The flat lands and pocosin borders produced grasses for cattle grazing and nuts and masts for hog foraging.

A few grants exceeded the maximum square mile as limited by law and others generally were large. One Henry Hackley, it is noted, acquired 800 acres in one piece, which included Scratch Hall Branch on old Sarem Creek Road, south of Taylor's Mill Pond. Henry Baker patented near Hackley on Horsepen Pocosin and acquired other tracts in Chowan and Bertie counties. John Webb and Stephen Eure patented most of the fertile Fort Island land. John Pipkin obtained a large site upon the Chowan River and extensive pine barren holdings in the north of Hall.

By the end of the eighteenth century, however, most of these and other large holdings had been subdivided, but at the same time new estates were building by purchase.

The bounty on naval stores instituted in 1705 by the English Parliament apparently added to the value of these pine forests. A trade in tar, pitch and turpentine soon

[109]

developed; and for a century and a half this provided the area's chief industry.

In 1728, a few miles north on the Virginia-Carolina border, William Byrd explained it had grown customary for the inhabitants to "pick up Knots of Lightwood in Abundance, which they burn into tar, and then carry it to Norfolk or Nansimond for a Market." Although this tar burned cordage, he said, for other purposes it was as good as that made in Sweden or Muscovy.

In the same tar-producing country Byrd found "all the Marks of Poverty, being for the most Part Sandy and full of Pines. This kind of Ground, tho' unfit for Ordinary Tillage, will however bring Cotton and Potatoes in Plenty, and Consequently Food and Rainment to such as are easily contented, and, like the Wild Irish, find more Pleasure in Laziness than Luxury."

This country, added Byrd, also could produce Indian corn; and the more industrious "make what Quantity of tar they please, tho' indeed they are not always sure of a Market for it."

The tar makers were at liberty to remove lightwood timbers from the untaken lands much like livestock owners for decades had utilized the King's acres for open range. Boxing of the pine tree for turpentine extraction quickly became common in Carolina. In 1738 Henry McCulloch said it had been "a practice of long standing in the Colony for people to Box pine trees for Turpentine and burn light wood for Pitch and Tarr without taking out Pattents for the Lands." The same practice prevailed for shingle making until late in the nineteenth century.

The production of naval stores required the services of coopers to make barrels, and within a few years there developed in the Albemarle area an export market for pipe-staves, barrel-staves and hogshead-staves. The white oak and red oak, present in abundance, were used in their manufacture. Whiteoak Pocosin, apparently named for the prevalence of this tree, lay upon the Hall area.

An export trade in shingles coincided with the development of the stave market.

By the middle of the eighteenth century local markets for naval stores had developed. In 1755 inspectors were appointed at Bennetts Creek bridge and at Maul's farm on the Chowan River for these and other export commodities. By 1770 inspectors were appointed at Winton on the Chowan and at Mount Sion on Potecasi Creek near the Meherrin and Chowan rivers.

Traffic in naval stores to the Nansemond and Norfolk markets overland by this time had been limited largely to the eastern area along the Dismal Swamp. At most, two barrels of tar, pitch or turpentine could be carried on a cart, and a two-team wagon would carry no more than twice that.

Water transportation was more convenient. The barrels could be loaded on flats or rolled into the water, bound into rafts and floated to deep-water landings or distilleries.

The Mount Sion landing, established by some Scotch merchants before the middle of the eighteenth century, provided representative accomodations. It had a mansion with a store and outhouses, constructed on "a healthy eminence" which sloped downward to a "flatt."

Before the end of the eighteenth century Cyprian Cross had opened a store at The Cross near the fork of the Winton and Barfields roads where he could cater to both the local trade and interstate travelers. Other stores were operated in the area of The Cross most of the nineteenth century.

The production of naval stores required a large amount of cheap labor in spring and summer when the plantations were at the peak of their activity. Poor whites and free Negroes were generally employed.

Few slaves were owned in the pine barrens, but some

Gathering the Pine Resin

men seem to have employed them. In 1790 Isaac Pipkin had 34, James Bradley 17 and Cyprian Cross 10. More than half of the Hall families owned no slaves and few of these owned more than one or two.

Turpentine, the natural juice of the pine tree, was obtained by cutting a half-moon shaped box in the tree near the ground from December to March and cornering once and "hacking" about six times from early spring until November. The juice dripped into the box and was dipped out and contained in barrels which had been spread about the forest at convenient intervals.

When old boxed trees were left standing, or those deadened by fire, the wood became saturated with pitchy matter called "light-wood." This was useful for kindling, a substitute for candles among the poor, and a source of tar.

Most of the pine forests had been used up before the Civil War, except for large quantities of "light-wood" from dead trees for tar making.

Tradition remembers Daniel Eure as one of the last large tar makers. He owned the land from Marsh Swamp to Story Brothers on U. S. 13, and "Daniel Eure's Tar Pit Ridge" still is a local landmark. Eure made tar before the Civil War, fought for the Confederacy, and returned home to make tar for a number of years afterwards.

A frolic usually took place when Eure and other tar makers burned their kilns. People of the neighborhood would gather at night, drink, talk, fight dogs, and sometimes wrestle and fight among themselves.

The kiln, which required great care to prevent it catching too much air and burning up, provided an atmosphere of excitement. Prof. H. E. Colton said in 1770:

"Few sights have in them more of somber grandeur than a large tar kiln at night. Its immense columns of slowly ascending smoke are now and then illumined by the leaping forth of a tongue of flame.

Firing the Tar Kiln

The wild cries of the men in the efforts to cover it quickly with earth add to the wildness of the scene."

Livestock, Drovers and Rustlers

The Hall area, with its extensive flatlands and pocosins to provide both grazing and natural fencing, was suited to livestock production; and until recent years almost every family had a few hogs and cows and a horse, sheep, goat or two.

Most of the meat was consumed fresh at home. Scarceness and cost of salt limited the amount which was brined, and little of this was sold.

Passing of the drover herds from south of the Chowan and Roanoke rivers along the main roads of Hall was a common spectacle until late in the nineteenth century. Strays from the endless herds passing through helped to populate the country with wild hogs and cows. These animals and a subtle form of rustling supported some of the area's poor.

Mention of "cowpen," "horsepen," and "hog pen" in the early records of Chowan and Gates counties suggests that from early colonial times such enclosures were used in the Hall area to protect the livestock from both wild animals and thieves.

Such losses were a major problem of the frontier and warranted laws to encourage destruction of marauding animals and control of "idle and disorderly persons."

In 1726 John Council and William Bryan were complaining that "Thomas Jones and others have Killed and destroyed great quantities of their Stocks Ranging on the Borders of this government."

A 1728 law made it necessary to leave ears on hides of wild cattle killed to prove the animals bore no ownership brands.

A 1745 act observed there were great numbers of people in the province "who have no settled Habitation, nor visible Method of Supplying themselves, by Industry or Honest Calling, many of whom come in from Neighboring Colonies, without proper passes, and kill Deer at all Seasons of the Year, and often leave the Carcasses in the woods and also steal and destroy cattle, and carry away Horses, and commit other Enormities . . ." These practices and burning of the range and fences were noted in 1766.

Rustling in ante-bellum Hall usually was practiced within the law. The Spencer Gang is mentioned in lore as a family which acquired land bordering a heavily traveled causeway. Cur-like dogs were said to have been trained to scatter the drover herds into the pocosins. When the drovers had gathered up what animals they could and continued their drive, members of the gang hunted down and slaughtered the strays as their table needed them.

Tradition adds, local strife developed when these people began killing stock indiscriminately from the open range. A neighbor, whose name has been forgotten, openly charged them with livestock theft, and soon afterwards as he walked through a lonely forest the ferocious dogs were set upon him. He sought to escape into the pocosins but was hunted down and shot to death.

Crude accomodations were provided for the drovers and their herds along some of the heavily traveled intercolonial ways. Barfields road, which crossed the Chowan River two miles southeast of Winton and joined the Winton road four miles northeast, was the chief traditional drover way from Carolina to the Norfolk, Virginia, market. After about a century and a half of service, in 1885 the river ferry was discontinued and the three-mile-long pocosin causeway left to the exclusive use of local hunters and fishermen.

It has been learned from John Crawford and Ben Godwin that the Barfields ferry flat was enclosed by a fence as high as a cow's back and zig zag rail fences stretched along the sides of the causeway. High rails also kept the driven animals from the quagmires at the pop-up bridge over the pocosin's Mud Creek.

An inn was located beside the roadway on 50-acre Little Island at the northeast end of the causeway. Almost a mile further onward beside the large sand ridge was the Road House — still standing up to a few years ago. This was a stable-like enclosure built in three sections to accomodate livestock overnight. Large out-swinging gates provided access to the stalls. Straw pallets and hay bedding were made available to the drovers, who remained with or close to the animals through the night. At times, it is said, they slept with their animals and others they lay beneath the open sky.

Barfields and some of the other ferries appear to have catered to the drover business. Some like nearby Winton, which was on the great wagon road out of Suffolk and was traveled by the stage coach, did not. Its causeway had neither fences to keep the drover herds from the bogs and wilds of the pocosins nor a road house.

Flush Times Befo' de Wah

The delight the Gates County plantation slave took in fabilizing the provincial fighting folks of Scratch Hall is represented in the September 22, 1899, "The Economist" of Elizabeth City by Dr. Thomas M. Riddick of Woodville, writing as "Sam Sawbones."

"Down on the plantation in Pasquotank, said Riddick, "there lives the faithful old body servant of my father" who occasionally "comes up to see me." The old fellow lived in the past and seemed ever in a mood to reminisce. "The delight of my life is to warm him up with a glass of life-giving elixir, and a good dinner, and then listen to him tell of 'flush times befo de War. . . .'

"Once upon a time he told me of a battle royal that took place among a crowd of beligerent Scratch Hallians who visited Gates Court for a little fistic entertainment—just as the festive Irishmen go to Donny Brook Fair. He assured me that although the presiding judge was seated upon the hotel piazza (United States Hotel) in order that he might over-awe evil doers by the majesty and dignity of his aug-ust presence, that he saw fourteen Scratch Hall men select a partner each, put off and go into the pugal-istic mill, where the tactics of Corbett and Sullivan were wholly distanced. And he continued: 'An Boss de fit and de fit, roun mong de boxes and barrels, twell de whole groun were kivered wid gouged out eyeballs dat lok des lak so many fox grapes.'

"But, Andrew, said I, were there no severed arms and legs in that carnival of Mars?

" 'No sah, he said, not one, fer Scratch Hall man always pinks fer de eye fus thing.' "

Country of One-Membered Men

One of the better known Scratch Hall fables claims that in olden times 'all the men of the section were one-mem-bered because of engaging in "no-holds-barred" fights. It was impossible for a traveler in those parts to find a native who did not have an eye, an arm, a leg or an ear missing.

Once when a Hertford County man announced he planned to take a trip through Scrach Hall, he was told by a friend he should choose another route. It was too dangerous to travel through that country of one-eyed people.

The Hertford man took the warning lightly and started on his journey. He ferried the Chowan River, traversed the wide river swamp and emerged on

[118]

sandy Bar Road. A few hundred yards along the way he met a man who spoke cordially enough, but he had only one eye. A short distance more another cordial passerby also had just one eye. The traveler stopped and pondered upon his friend's advice, decided the hazard was too great to continue further, and returned home.

A Family Feud

Tradition states that some Hall people faulted each other for any one of many reasons and that this led to frequent family feuds. According to one well known fable:

In the far-back years two children of two neighbor families living on Bar Road commenced to fight early one morning. As the day wore on other members joined until everyone down to the toothless grandparents were scrapping.

The feuders fought with any-and-everything they could pick up. As the day's sun sank into the Chowan River swamp the feuders were swinging the last of the unbroken fence rails.

Fighters of Skill

Any kind of fight was a delight in Scratch Hall, from a savage snarling-dog fang-slashing to a friendly contest between men to demonstrate their skill and daring. The greater the measure of excitement provided, the better.

Everyone was accomodating when arranging a fight. Thus no fights were without an audience. The swamp and ridge dwellers were on hand at the appointed time. Such was the case with the gun duel at Harrell's store soon after the Civil War.

Storekeeper Harrell and Elisha Parker had nothing against each other except their target shooting hadn't shown who was the better pistol marksman.

One day as a crowd had gathered at the store and ardorously debated the question the two men agreed nothing was left but to resolve the argument with a pistol duel—with each one the other's target. They would try to draw blood without inflicting a wound.

The spectators stood breathless as the duelists took turns at throwing pistol balls closer and closer to each other's head.

Eventually, after several near misses, Harrell grazed the base of Parker's nose and drew blood. The duel ended and Harrell was proclaimed the winner.

Scratch Hall Dog Lore

Those little log houses sitting about the Scratch Hall home were not dog kennels. There was no need to pamper the raw-bonish wolf-like curs with such accomodations. The outdoors was made for them, and it was just as wrong to let one indoors as it was to feed him before the hunt.

So the dogs were permitted to run as free as the wild creatures, except during persimmon-falling time, as a traditional story explains:

Scratch Hall dogs, like their masters, were persimmon eaters, and they had to be kept up during the autumn persimmon falling season.

The informed traveler could determine the number of dogs which belonged to each homestead just by counting the number augur holes in the cabin doors, for there was one hole for each dog.

After the night's hunt it was customary for the master to pull each dog's tail through a hole and tie a knot in it. Next morning, when the persimmons which had fallen during the night had been picked up, the dog was released.

Scratch Hall people were proud of their dogs. Each and every cur, in the eyes of his master, had some quality unexcelled by other dogs. Some could whip anything in the woods; some had "extra-scentsory" powers on the trail; and others had cultivated voices to make hunting pure deilght.

Mr. Franklin's Old Zeke, according to W. Frank Landing in his "War Cry of the South," was one of the extraordinary dogs:

"He was th' damnedest coon dog anywhere 'roun the parts. He was so old, musta been twenty years old, during th' day he could hardly go, but soon as the sun went down old Zeke would come alive. He'd get on th' trail of a coon and keep his nose on her trail 'till he treed her. You could hear old Zeke baying for miles 'round."

Old Jack Blount explained only one dog kennel was built in Scratch Hall "behin' de wah."

This was because one housewife demanded the augur holes in the doors to her home be plugged up to keep the witches from coming through, and she was so insistent that her husband was unable to overrule her.

Thus a log dog kennel was constructed to keep up the dogs during the persimmon falling time. After that, the disgruntled husband claimed that his dogs had been ruined from keeping them indoors. They no longer had their normal ardor on the trail.

The Scratch Hall Fisherman

The Scratch Hall fisherman remained quaint in his habits until good roads and the bridge over the Chowan River at Winton began to bring him out of isolation.

His boat was the dugout canoe, which when not in use was hidden in some swamp creek to snooze away in the wilds much like Rip Van Winkle.

Watching and Preying – by Porte Crayon

His fish traps were after the Indian design, only constructed by improved methods. White oak splits of various sizes were fashioned into weirs for use the year around. These were especially useful during the herring and shad spawning season when they served much like today's Dutch nets. An assortment of cages were anchored on the bottom of streams as trap lines.

The more spectacular fisherman was the hook and line fellow who idled upon the water as if he had nothing else to do. In 1857 Porte Crayon pictured a sleeping fisherman upon the upper Chowan and remarked,

"ah, there is a living wight at last! a native Carolinian under his own beaming sun, lying in a canoe watching his fish trap after the Southern fashion, while the sagacious eagle, with contemptuous aduacity, settles down and carries off his prey."

Mills Eure, Strong-Arm Politician

As Hall Township's Mills Eure wished, says tradition, so went Hall politically almost a quarter of a century before the Civil War and as long afterwards.

Eure was said to have possessed the power of wealth, the gift of oratory and the carriage of a plantation master, all of which he used in necessary proportions to control the popular elctorate.

Eure's wealth included several large farms in Hall and Reynoldson townships plus extensive turpentine holdings in these townships and in Georgia.

His oratory was emotion-stirring—silver-tongued or stump-fighting, precisely tailored to suit the occasion.

A large part of his following was "very poor people" before whom he subtly represented himself as "a very rich and a very strong man." He was seldom seen with currency; he, instead, "kept his money in gold coins" which he handled rather carelessly except when engaging in a business deal or hiring a hand.

During Eure's later years "a big old pipe" with a long stem lent individualism to his firm face and greying hairs. He was constantly packing this close companion with fresh tobacco. The tobacco was carried loose in a pocket with any number of gold coins; and should poor men, women or children be near, a gold coin might be seen to go into the pipe with the tobacco.

Thus Eure helped others create the fable that he was so rich that he smoked gold pieces.

A "Bill Teaser," a high beaver hat, was a companion as constant as his pipe; and it, too, won a place in local lore.

Eure's domineering attitude apparently accounted for some of his bitter enemies. One of these was one Matthews who came to odds with Eure over a now long-forgotten incident.

The two men are said to have exchanged bitter words as Eure stopped in front of Matthews' gate. Matthews became so infuriated that he seized a rail from the roadside fence and swung at Eure's head. The blow caught the hat and knocked it into the road, and unscathed Eure promptly urged his horse and stick gig from the scene.

The land and political baron did not relinquish protective custody over his former slaves after the Civil War, and they seemed to value his wise and firm guidance. Thus it was only normal when one Sunday morning, learning two of his husky Negroes had been fighting, Eure interceded. He pulled them apart, gave each a drink of brandy and "made them kiss and make up."

Ken Lawrence's store at the present site of Eure Christian Church two miles east of the village of Eure was the customary place for the boss' political rallies.

"A peck bucket of whiskey" was one of the attractions, and invariably large crowds of men attended. The speaking got started after the bucket with a dipper in it was placed on a stump and the host had cried gustily, "Come up boys and help yourself!"

Eure, by no means, was the first Hall politician to mix strong drink with politics. Long before his rise to power, political rallies of the area were being called "Hard Cider Meetings."

Mrs. Linda Jordan Hofler says one of the fables explaining the origin of the name "Scratch Hall" is linked with these old rallies.

In the old days, it was generally reported, free apple brandy was used to bring the voters from the woods and swamps. And in Hall opposing political parties assembled at the same time and place. One group would gather on one side of the road and their opponents, on the other.

A single cider jug was brought out and set down in the middle of the road, and friends of different political leanings took turns at it. Meanwhile, a speaker mounted a stump on one side of the road and an opponent took his turn on a stump on the other side. The speakers shouted "fighting words" and the brandy prepared their listeners for combat. Small fights grew into bigger ones, until there was one big free-for-all.

The electorate went home from the more successful rallies with fewer eyes, noses, ears, fingers, arms and legs.

The rallies of those old days, however, never produced so colorful a politician as Mills Eure, who let it be clearly known "all my friends" and all who drank Mills Eure's wiskey voted as Mills Eure wished.

He who voted otherwise or failed to show at election day suffered Mills Eure's displeasure, which could lead to economic recourse . . . and some whispered, "violence."

Eure was "an irrepressible orator" to a correspondent

of "The Economist" of Elizabeth City who reported the Gates County Democratic Convention of June 1878.

The county, in conformance with tradition, was divided by "contending clans" which made the event "a boisterous session" starting at 1 p.m. and continuing "until the shades of night were falling . . ."

Eure and several other speakers spoke "not once, but often and well." Henry Willey sought to "pour oil on the troubled waters and smooth the wrinkled front of war," but his "words of wisdom, moderation and peace" went unheeded; the oil caught fire. "A taunt from Young America, that Old America has become obsolete" and intimation "ANTE BELLUM notions" were to be discounted relit "fires of departed youth in the breast of the gray-haired statesman" who rushed into "a drawn battle— with much wind, but no blood" with the "infatuated youth."

When at last a vote was reached the chair announced the "noes" had it. Immediately "the corpulent hero of Scratch Hall is on his feet, stern determination is written on his face, wrath quivering in his eye, and his stentorian voice rings out clear and distinct above the din of bustle . . . 'Mr. Chairman, in the name of Scratch Hall, I object to the snap judgment you have taken on us. I'll be d . . . . . if this fellow sitting by me didn't vote twice. He said "NO! NO!" I demand a division.' "

The "noes" still had the vote after the granted division; and a brisk skirmish" ensued with "various dilatory motions." Eventually the opposing candidate "sweeps the stakes." Then came "a truce, a parley, and apologies for the hot words spoken in debate, a hand shaking . . ."

Survival of the Log Boat

CHAPTER XI

The Native Boat Builders

Along the swampy borders of the Chowan River, where the cypress tree lorded the forest, woodsmen practiced the art of log boat building until early in the twentieth century. Their boats, fashioned basically after the Indian log canoe, were scooped with hand tools from large logs in many sizes — as canoes, perreaugers and flats . . . . even one steamboat.

Traditional skill was demonstrated both by the Indian and the Englishman in designing and creating a craft of such fine balance as to make it capable to carry with ease burdens upon the broad—sometimes stormy—sounds and rivers of old Albemarle area.

Arthur Barlowe, while exploring the Carolina coast in 1584, paused to admire the manner by which the Indian made his boat of the pitch pine tree. The savage, he said, either burned down a great tree or made free use of one which had been felled by the wind. He applied, "gum and rosin" to its surface to feed a charring fire, and then the log was carefully and tediously shaped into a boat hulk by scraping down the burned portion with shells. The hulk, by use of like devices, was scooped out.

Some of the Indian's log boats were so large that they could carry twenty men, Barlowe explained. The Indian propelled such dugouts with oars fashioned like scoops or—when the water was not too deep—with poles.

In 1587, after exploring inland to the Chowan River

region where the waters were bordered by large cypress swamps, Thomas Hariot noted that the cypress also was made into boats "with the help of fire, hatchets of stone and shells." This timber was "great, tall, straight, soft, light . . ."

Three-quarters of a century later when other Englishmen pushed southward from Virginia and established their homes about the Albemarle Sound and its many tributaries these waters provided the natural highways of the new country, and the log boat became the chief vehicle of local commerce and travel upon them.

Absence of good roads made boats of great value indeed. Except some half-dozen intercolonial trails, roads received little attention for more than two centuries, and people of the old County of Albemarle area continued to rely chiefly on boats—enlarged or designed to meet changing needs and propelled by oars, poles, sails and steam.

The planter, like the Indian, found the pine and the cypress trees best for building his log boats. As the eighteenth century opened John Lawson proclaimed the value of the great cypress, a tree which reached thirty-six feet in circumference. He said:

". . . Of these great Trees the Pereaugers and Canoes are scooped and made, which sort of Vessels are chiefly to pass over the Rivers, Creeks, and the Bays, and to transport Goods and Lumber from one river to another. Some are so large as to carry thirty Barrells, though of one entire Piece of Timber. Others are split down the Bottom and a piece added thereto, will carry eighty or an hundred. Several have gone out our Inlets on the Ocean to Virginia, laden with Pork and other Produce of the Country. "

Lawson said that a man and his son decked a canoe capable of carrying sixteen barrels and considered it so

INDIANS MAKING CANOE—de Bry after John White

seaworthy that the man "brought her to the Collectors to be cleared for the Barbadoes. The officer, however, regarded him as "a Man that had lost his Senses, and argued the Danger and Impossibility of performing such a Voyage in a hollow tree . . ."

A quarter of a century later Dr. Brickell stated that dugouts generally were made of cypress and equipped with paddles, oars and masts "according to their size and bigness." As vehicles of commerce:

"Some of these Periaugers are so large that they are capable of carrying forty or fifty barrels of Pitch or Tar. In these Vessels likewise they carry Goods, Horses, and other Cattle from one plantation to another over large and spacious Rivers; they frequently trade in them to Virginia and other places on the continent, no Vessel of the same Burthen

[129]

made after the European manner is able to out Sail one of these Periaugers."

Brickell said the canoe, smaller of the log boats, sometimes was made to carry "only two or three men." Indians and Englishmen, men and women alike, were skilled in managing the canoes.

Boats were so important to the colonial Carolinian that the Assembly enacted severe laws against their theft. A 1715 act provided a fine of forty shillings for stealing one; and if the offender refused to pay, a justice of peace could set him in stocks and have him publicly whipped up to twenty lashes. A slave or servant breaking the law could be whipped in like manner.

Small Boats Help Hinterland to Develop

The small log boat and the shallow draught flat made possible development of many plantations which had no frontage on the large creeks and rivers and harborage for commercial sails trading with New England and the West Indies.

A canal or small waterway enabled the canoes, pereaugers and flats to move naval stores, staves, shingles and produce to points of call of the sloops, schooners, brigantines, brigs, and—after 1836—steam boats, and return to the land-locked plantations with goods.

A few deep-water landings and no less than five small creeks made the log boat especially serviceable to the western area of Gates County. Both quaint customs and an adequate supply of large trees enabled the dugout to remain the chief water vehicle along the Chowan River's eastern swamp border until the beginning of the twentieth century.

Manner of Nineteenth Century Dugout Building

Some of the craftsmen who built dugouts survived until a few years ago. One was John Crawford, who told of how he and three other men built a 19½-foot-long boat.

His brother Henry Crawford planned for twenty feet, but the large cypress felled in Sarem Creek Swamp had a wind-shake which necessitated a six-inch reduction.

Two skilled woodsmen, Rufus Harrell and Frank Landing, helped the two brothers. The hulk was shaped with axes and drawing knives, a task which required both a right-handed and left-handed man to draw the curves on both sides.

A dozen or more augur holes then were cut into the hulk—about the sides and bottom The men took a coopers adz and round sleeve to dig out and smooth down the inside to the tip of pegs which had been inserted into the augur holes as thickness gauges. Permanent pegs then closed the holes. A narrow strip of gunneling was affixed about the top edges of the boat to absorb solid blows and to prevent the shell from splitting where the wood had been cut across the grain.

It was another task to move the boat one-half mile through the swamp to the creek. A northeast storm sent both the Chowan's tides and the Crawford brothers and two strong men, George Williams and Richard Green, into the swamp—also a quart of apple brandy. The men were drammed with the brandy, and the dugout moved slowly through muck and across water pools to the creek. More drams—the boat was on a nine-mile journey down the creek and up the Chowan River to mooring at Ray's Beach.

A gale swept the surface of the river into a sea of whitecaps. The ambitious oarsmen sent the boat's bow plowing through the waves—until instructed to slow down and permit the long curvacious craft to ascend and descend to the symphony of the water.

Hall men were accustomed to travel great distances on their dugouts. Few were willing to pay passage on river steamers for the sixty-mile round-trip to Franklin, Virginia, and the seventy-five-mile round-trip to Edenton. Two good oarsmen, leaving early in the morning, could attend to their business and be home by early night.

Hall natives still remember adventuring with their fathers upon the river—the thrill of passing steamers, with strange faces at their rails, "plowing out the river" and cradling their small boats upon the waves rolling shoreward.

The Dugout Steamer "Tadpole"

The colonial pereauger, the skillfully designed commercial log boat, had long disappeared from the Chowan River when two Gates County brothers constructed the rarest log boat of all — a dugout steamboat.

J. A. Ramsey of Winton told of its recent completion in the March 21, 1878, "The Inquirer" of Murfreesboro. It had been launched and given the name "Tadpole," supposedly because of its dimunitive size. Althought the boat had visited Winton three times Ramsey hadn't seen it, but he had learned it was scheduled to ply the Meherrin and Chowan Rivers.

About six weeks later, on April 30, "The Economist" of Elizabeth City told its readers, the steamer " 'Tadpole' is afloat and doing a lively business."

The strange craft had been built upon "one of the bleak Sand-hills on the Chowan" at the Dowry near Gatlington by Duke and Tom Story "who had scarcely ever seen the inside of a steamboat in their lives." It was explained that they had taken a notion they wanted a boat and "just went along and built it" with no outside assistance.

Nonetheless, the "Tadpole" was a "smart trick" which

reflected "high credit upon the energy and pluck of these rising young men." The forty-foot-long boat had been dug out of three pine logs and fitted with a five-horsepower engine. Used as a tugboat, the dugout "tows a barge with 2500 oak R. R. ties from Gatlington (a small river settlemen with a wharf and stave mill) to Franklin."

Traditional sources explain that two logs provided the two sides of the steamer and a third one was fitted as its center section. The three parts were secured together by mortising and pegging. Strong gunneling and bracing timbers gave the hull its necessary structural strength.

The little boat had an advantage over larger ones because it could navigate many of the larger creeks serving the rivers. Thus on May 28 "The Economist" states the boat, with Major William Daughtry on board, had made a prospecting trip ten miles up Somerton Creek "with the view of opening up a trade in the benighted region bordering this stream." The skipper was pleased with prospects of a profitable trade, especially in lumber.

Although the little boat and her crew of two operated on the Chowan, Blackwater and Meherrin rivers more than twenty years, she was no outstanding success. After a few years the Story brothers sold her to Camp Manufacturing Company of Franklin, Virginia, and then she was used chiefly to tow rafts of logs from narrow waters.

Some of the last log boats on the upper Chowan River were made of hollow cypress trees and used by lumbermen of the Somerton Creek area. Canoes and flats were easily made by dressing off one side of the hollow log and attaching ends fashioned from boards. These boats, easy to capsize, commonly were used in pairs or fours as raft helpers and as utility craft.

DESCENT INTO DISMAL SWAMP ON U. S. 158

PART 4

The Wonderful Dismal Swamp

CHAPTER XII

Origin Still Holds Mysteries

Traveling eastward across Gates County, North Carolina, and Nansemond County, Virginia, the gently rolling plain suddenly drops off fifteen to twenty feet as if were descending into a great river valley.

Farms and farm homes familiar to the countryside for endless miles suddenly disappear. They can go no further against the bold barrier—one of America's natural wonders—which lies ahead.

A new plain — first as a vast, varied and mysterious bog reluctant to disclose its boundless secrets — resumes a slow and tedious descent. It drops a few inches each mile as it moves eastward towards the Atlantic Ocean; northeast, Hampton Roads; and the southeast, the Albemarle Sound.

The spectacle is the Great Dismal Swamp which offers visible evidence that nature has toiled here through trackless ages and that her work is still far from complete.

She remains unconquored after man has whittled at her borders for three centuries, and within her wilds jungle rule among both plants and animals occupy them with an endless struggle for daily food and a new sunrise.

This complex lady, so skillfully fashioned, has been adorned by jeweled phrases by her admirers:

"dismal or great Desart;"

"inhospitable bog;"

"dark and gloomy with sombre grandeur;"

"weird and wonderful jungle;"

"brooding quagmire shrouded in mystery;"

"a dreadful swamp of vast extent;"

"a vast quagmire yielding or quaking on the surface to the tread of man;"

"rank, impenetrable, riotous with exoitic blossoms and foilage in summer and grotesque with gnarled tree - trunks and twisted limbs and ghostly gray stumps standing lonely in the marshes in winter;"

"one of the most unique natural wonders of the world;"

"a sanctuary for everything hideous and dreadful."

Geologists say an ancient shallow sea once extended to the western border of Dismal Swamp. And there arises from one's imagination the roar of cresting waves dashing themselves against a sandy beach where jungles now begin.

The sea was the last of several which at various times during the geologic calendar encroached upon the coastal plains.

This particular sea, it is explained, came at the conclusion of the last great ice age when melting glaciers released vast quantities of water into the seas of the world and sent their levels bounding upward. Subsequent glacial formation has shrunk the seas to their present level.

The Talbot Terrace lies here. Not as a wonder to see; it is hidden as semi-solidified beds of shells and skeletons of marine animals some ten feet beneath mucky ooze, quicksands and root-matted swamp floors. However, a reminder of its presence lies upon the canal banks where such remains have been rolled to the surface.

Even though some records of Great Dismal's birth and

development are distinctly inscribed, she is so secretive that she has either left some parts unclear or omitted them altogether. Thus she has sent geologists toiling to reach agreement as to how she actually came about.

Their task is far from complete. Her awesome tangles suggest she may have grown slowly from the clogging of drainage through vegetation. Or she may not have been so contrary as expected and emerged—like most morasses—as the remains of an old lagoon or sound shut off from the sea by a barrier beach which shaped her into a depression.

Mother of Legends

Little wonder Great Dismal is the source of many legends — even the one with a large helping of imagination which claims that Lief Erickson and his hardy Norsemen sailed into her fastness about the year 1000.

Unlike most great swamps, Great Dismal is fed by a small watershed—a few branches and creeks reaching ten to fifteen miles westward. Yet from some place—the sky or the earth—she wells forth enough water to sog down her deep floor—except during extended droughts—and to feed seven rivers which creep from her choking tangles and promptly broaden nobly for dramatic entry into the broad waters of the Albemarle and Currituck sounds and Hampton Roads.

Rivers Betray Mother Dismal

Yet these very rivers Mother Dismal nourishes so devotedly have contributed to her partial undoing. They have permitted an assault upon her with canals and drainage ditches from the east, northeast and southeast—until her onetime 2,200 square miles of swamplands, which comprised the greater part of several counties, have now shrunk to about 750 square miles.

[137]

So by changing our course and traveling westward the houses, rich blackland farms and dry rank forests stand as modern milestones to man's conquest of her resources.

Nonetheless, those 750 square miles which remain of Great Dismal comprise her vitals, her great wilderness untouched except by the shingle-getters, lumbermen and peat fires.

Rich and Varied Plantlife

The evergreen juniper forests with quivering floors carpeting peat beds; the dark, mucky and wet black gum swamps; impenetrable thickets of bush, reed and vine jungles make her still one of the wildest places in eastern America.

She is thirty-seven miles long and ranges to twelve miles wide. About sixty per cent of her area lies in Gates, Perquimans, Pasquotank, Camden and Currituck counties in North Carolina; and forty per cent in Nansemond and Norfolk counties, Virginia.

She contains about thirty-five kinds of trees, including cypress, juniper, red maple, loblolly pine, water ash, poplar, sweet gum, holly and wild cherry. The cypress is the most notable. Many old stumps of gigantic size tell of the primeval forest while there still are specalments 120 feet high and four to five feet in diameter at the swoolen base.

Botanists divide the swamp into two principal formations. The black gum or dark swamp is covered with a heavy deciduous forest; and the black gum is in great part a virgin formation. The light or open juniper swamp, originally the greater part covered with an evergreen forest, is now in many places almost barren of trees and bears a growth of shrubs, cane, fern and peat moss.

The juniper swamp is not so wet as the black gum swamp, and juniper reproduces rapidly. Frequently fires, however, prevent a material increase in these trees.

Cane brakes cover extensive areas. Woody bamboo, known locally as reeds, often tower to fifteen feet.

Vines make parts of the swamp impenetrable. The woody liana embrace the trunks and often climb to tops of trees. Common are supple jack or rattan, yellow jessamine, cross vine, poison ivy and muscadine grape.

Wildlife Sanctuary

Great Dismal is one of the last great natural wildlife sanctuaries in the east. Still abundant are the black bear, deer, wildcat, raccoon, opossum, mink, weasel, otter, muskrat, fox, rabbit and squirrel.

About seventy-five species of birds include warblers and cormorants, doves, woodpeckers, and ospreys. Waterfowl come in winter.

In the reptile family are three poisonous snakes—the rattlesnake, copperhead and cottonmouth moccasin—and about twelve non-poisonous varieties. Abundant also are lizards, turtles and skinks.

Lake Drummond, located near the center of the swamp. is fished for pike, perch, pickerel and several other fish types. Small ponds hidden in the fastness of the swamp and the network of canals also contain fish.

Viewpoint Constantly Changes

Man's viewpoint of Great Dismal's beauty and usefulness have been changing constantly since the first Englishman began to reshape the Indian's forests to the needs of his slowly spawning civilization.

Until this pioneer axeman had rolled back large open spaces into the highland forests Great Dismal was not regarded as a wildlife sanctuary—only a mysterious place where only the Indian huntsman dared to journey in autumn or where weak Indian groups retired to a hidden haven from militant pressures of neighbors and there endured jungle-like hardships.

To the Englishman this was a terra incognita—as perhaps the vast wilderness was to the Indian when spring and summer foilage drew a shady curtain. As such it was an antipodes both to the Englishman and the Indian wherein all sorts of terrors—from fire-breathing monsters to Hades-like phantoms- -dwelled.

From unseen recesses the peat fires, gnawing at old vegetable matter beneath the swamp floor, spewed forth a stenching yellow smoke pall. As the wind wished it was sent drifting for miles about to tell both the Indian and the Englishman there was a real basis for their wild tales.

Economically, Great Dismal was valueless to the early settlers except for the reeds it produced for their cattle. So long as rich lands were to be had upon the watercourses it was one big waste to be avoided.

At times the great morass did prove of service to some travelers. Its high western rim, which defined the border of the ancient sea, kept the old Indian trail following it devotedly dry from the Nansemond River in Virginia to the Albemarle Sound in Carolina. It proved as great a hindrance to the traveler who journeyed around its eastern wilds, for it forced him to pass over wide rivers and to go almost to the Currituck Sound to make his way to the Norfolk, Virginia, area.

Great Dismal Swamp is the larger of several dismals which extend intermittently across the lower plains of North Carolina. All of these seem to have been regarded as "deserts" by the early settlers, for Thomas Pollock described one graphically as such in 1713 as the Tuscarora War was terminating:

"If (King Tom) Blount (of the Tuscaroras) keep the peace, we shall have only the Mattamuskeets and

[140]

Core Indians to mind, who of late have done us great mischief, having killed and taken of our people . . . about 45 at Croatan Roanoke Island, and Alligator River, there being about 50 or 60 men of them got together between Matchepungo River and Roanoke Island which is about 100 miles in length and of considerable breadth, all in a manner lakes, quagmires, and Cane swamps, and is, I believe, one of the greatest deserts in the world, where it is impossible for white men to follow them. . . ."

Fifteen years afterwards, in 1728, William Byrd quotes a Mr. Wilson, who dwelled to the east of Great Dismal as calling it a "great Desart."

Byrd went on to dramatize the mysterious and "inhospitable" character of the great swamp — an acceptable view at the time—and received credit for giving the place a bad name. To him it was a "filthy Bogg," a "Dirty Place," and "an uncomfortable Habitation for any thing that has life." Its filthiness was so great that "Exhalations continually rise from this vast Body of mire and Nastiness infest the Air for many Miles around and render it very unwholesome for the Bordering inhabitants. It makes them liable to Agues, Pleurisies, and many other Distempers, that kill abundance of People, and make the rest look no better than Ghosts."

Meanwhile, Byrd weighed in his visions the possibility of utilizing the vast natural resources of the swamp. It could be drained and made to produce quantities of hemp, he stated in a proposal to organize a company and to obtain a grant from the Crown with quit rents and tax exemptions.

"Filthy Bogg" Becomes Healthful Legend
However, by the ante-bellum period Byrd's view of the swamp had been completely reversed. The brandy-brown

acid "juniper water" impregnated with the sap of juniper and cypress trees was considered healthful. Swampers said it was good for anything from rhematism to retardation of aging.

Sailing ships contemplating long voyages filled their casks with the water because it would not spoil quickly. Legend states that Blackbeard the pirate sailed near the headwaters of Dismal Swamp rivers to fill his casks and that Commodore Peary carried the swamp's water with him on his trip to Japan.

Eventually the swamp's water became a health legend. Robert Arnold said, "No one has ever died in Dismal Swamp from disease."

The water supposedly had a similar effect upon the swamp's wildlife and provided one explanation why at times the animals and reptiles grew into monsters.

Early in the nineteenth century people were convinced a health resort would develop around the swamp's lake. Lake Drummond Hotel was built on its brink and received patronage of "pleasuring parties" for a number of years.

Wine made from blackberries and wild cherries gathered from the swamp was so exhilirating that it too was called "juniper water."

Land Company Utilizes Resources

It was only natural as young America weighed visions of growth and development that keen minds should put the swamp in the economic balance. So did young George Washington who made his first visit to the Dismal in 1763 and returned five more times before the Revolution and involvement in politics claimed his interest. He acquired a 5,000-acre share in The Dismal Swamp Land Company, and he and his brother-in-law Fielding Lewis purchased jointly about 1100 acres of land in Perquimans (later Gates)

County, near Holley Grove, North Carolina.

Washington, as a young surveyor, concluded the entire Dismal Swamp could be drained and made into farm land. With this in mind he and his associates bought about 40,000 acres of swamplands and formed the Dismal Swamp Land Company. Some land was drained and tilled, but the profits were small.

After the Revolution the company turned to the production of juniper shingles, and this business boomed and netted large profits.

The Washington Ditch, cut five miles through the western side of the swamp to Lake Drummond by the land company was the Dismal's first canal. Tradition states that the young surveyor—the country's future first president—spaded the first shovel of dirt for the canal.

Washington Legends

Other Washington legends have sprung up around Dismal Swamp. When George came down to look after his plantation at Holley Grove in present Gates County he was said to have called on General Joseph Riddick and General Kedar Ballard. As he went down to examine the swamp he tied his horse at White Oak Spring and hid his whiskey in the hollow of a large oak which stood beside the spring until a few years ago. When he traveled around the southern border of the swamp he put up at the Eagle Tavern in Hertford. He fell in Deep Creek on his journey northward and exclaimed, "Oh! what a deep creek," thus giving it a name. Story tellers insist he had an active hand in building the Dismal Swamp Canal, and some are wont to give the waterway his name.

Prosperity of the shingle business induced the land company to construct the larger Jericho canal from the northern edge of Lake Drummond ten miles to Suffolk. This was four feet deep and adequate to transport shingles

WEIRD LAKE DRUMMOND—N. C. Department of
Conservation and Development photo

to a tidewater creek landing upon the Nansemond River where ocean-going vessels were loaded.

Swamp timber, consisting primarily of juniper, cypress and pine, also was removed from Great Dismal with heavy profits for the company.

The mining of the swamp forests of its resources was accomplished by use of a large number of Negroes. Some of these were owned by the land company as slaves and others were slaves hired from the nearby plantations.

Strange Lake With a Legend

Lake Drummond, locked in the weirdest and wildest part of Great Dismal, was found higher than the surrounding swamp by Washington. It still was known as Drummond's Pond, which legend explains was named after Carolina's first governor, William Drummond.

The age of the legend remains unknown, but an account of it reported in the January 1838 "Southern Literary Messenger" is essentially the same as told in later years. The lake was named "after the discoverer, who wandering in pursuit of game, with two companions, was lost, and in his ramblings, came upon the lake. His comrades failed to thread their way out. Drummond returned and gave an account of the sheet of water, which was accordingly called after him."

Drummond, Carolina's governor 1664-67, also was remembered as a martyr of the Indian wars. Virginia Governor William Berkeley had him hanged in 1677 for his part in Bacon's Rebellion.

Lore of Late Recording

Indian tales of late recording and contemporary English writings tell of a variety of monsters inhabiting the vitals of Dismal Swamp in both prehistoric and early historic times. Soon after 1700 a "North Briton," as recorded by William Byrd, was happy to escape the monsters and distresses of the vast unknown when he inadvisably went upon a dangerous discovery of it.

Meanwhile, witch, spirit and devil lore brought to the borders of Dismal Swamp by the English settlers was adapted to the new setting. Some stories seem to have been blended with Indian tales.

Seemingly, escapists began turning to Dismal Swamp as a sanctuary before the Revolution, for Isaac Weld reported that wild men were dwelling within the swamp late in the eighteenth century. Thence to the Civil War it was represented as a sanctuary for runaway slaves and outlaws. Midway the nineteenth century the Northern abolitionist press publicized it extensively as such. Harriet Beecher Stowe - expoited the interest and wrote an unrealistic novel about the hunted slave "Dred."

Sir Thomas Moore's 1803 ballard, "The Lake of Dismal Swamp," based on an Indian legend, awakened romantic interest in Dismal Swamp; and the nineteenth century is marked by the ascendancy of romantic notions—except upon the borders of the great morass where the people saw more mystery than romance in the treacherous wilderness and concerned themselves more with stories about the wildlife, personal experiences and fabulous tales accumulating over the years.

Last came the naturalist who found the fauna and flora of Great Dismal both rare and varied. To him it became one of nature's most charming sanctuaries and gardens.

Road and Canal Building

CHAPTER XIII

Great Dismal Beats Stubborn Retreat

It was more than a century after establishment of the permanent English colony at Jamestown, Virginia, before the first white man passed through Dismal Swamp. He is said to have been Samuel Swann, a practical surveyor with the North Carolina commission of 1728. While other commissioners went around the swamp and awaited on the opposite side, Swann and fellow workmen cut their way fifteen miles through the wilderness.

No significant explorations or assaults upon the swamp were made for another half-century when the Dismal Swamp Land Company was formed, cut the Washington Ditch to Lake Drummond, and began utilizing the swamp's resources.

About the same time Gideon Lamb made a significant contribution to travel about the eastern side of Dismal Swamp.

Lamb's Toll Road

By 1778 Lamb had bridged the upper Pasquotank River and laid a causeway through the Great Dismal Swamp between Pasquotank and Camden counties "at considerable Expense, only Aided by a small Subscription to the adjacent Inhabitants. . . ." He was allowed the same toll taken at Relfe's Ferry near present Elizabeth City. A year later the Assembly granted him permission to span Great Dismal between Pasquotank and Perquimans counties and charge a toll one-half that allowed for the ferry from Edenton to Duckingfield. The two undertakings eliminated two long ferry crossings and provided a shorter eastern route through two branches of the swamp to Norfolk, Virginia.

Traffic contemplated along "Lamb's Toll Road" was chiefly commercial, including horses, carriages, cattle, sheep and hogs.

The Dismal Swamp Canal

In 1787 and 1790 Virginia and North Carolina, respectively, passed acts incorporating the Dismal Swamp Canal Company which proposed to issue private stock to cut a canal from Pasquotank River in North Carolina to Elizabeth River in Virginia, but it was 1793 before slave gangs were set to work at both ends. George Washington became one of the first subscribers purchasing $500 in stock.

The canal bank was useful as a shortened toll road long before the canal was completed. Unanticipated obstacles delayed passage of the first vessel to June 1814; but the canal was not of much service until 1828 and after the federal government bought $200,000 in stock. The canal was made forty feet wide and capable of handling vessels of five and one-half foot draught. The water level was assured by a three and one-half-mile long feeder ditch from Lake Drummond.

Avenue to Lake Opened to Sightseers

Completion of the Jerico Canal from Suffolk to Lake Drummond in 1810 by the Dismal Swamp Land Company brought a tide of visitors and sightseers to the lake Moore had made famous. In 1838 a correspondent for the "Southern Literary Messenger" embarked upon "a board boat

A BARGE ON A DISMAL SWAMP CANAL
by Porte Crayon

called a periauger" at the land company's lumber yard
and was "pushed with poles, by two negroes, ten miles,
along a narrow canal" to the lake.

After a short period of prosperity the Dismal Swamp
Canal Company began to run into new difficulties. Construction of the Albemarle and Chesapeake Canal to the
east of it took some of its business and so did the new
railroads. The United States Government purchased it in
1929, and since that time it has been operated by the
Corps of Engineers.

Canals West of Dismal Swamp Planned

As the nineteenth century opened people to the west of Dismal Swamp began thinking of construction of canals to open up their area to commerce.

In 1791 an act of the Virginia Legislature was obtained to cut a canal from a branch of Nansemond River to Somerton Creek to provide an avenue to the Chowan River for such vessels as barges which were unsuited for navigating the broad waters of the Albemarle Sound. The idea was found impractical because of the elevation and broken nature of the intermediate land.

An alternate route was projected. This proposed to pass from Bennetts Creek, a tributary of the Chowan River, to the Nansemond River at Suffolk where "a precise level was found, except one or two places of very small extent." The North Carolina and Virginia legislatures of 1804-5 authorized a twenty-three and one-half mile canal, but the necessary funds for the project were not raised within the prescribed time.

With the Dismal Swamp Canal in successful operation and a feeder ditch leading from the canal to Lake Drummond, in 1829 the North Carolina General Assembly authorized the Lake Drummond and Orapeake Canal Company to cut a canal from Holley Grove to the lake and thus establish a water route from the western side of Dismal Swamp to Norfolk. The toll was to be half that of the Dismal Swamp Canal. Although the act came up in several subsequent legislatures with amendments, the canal was never constructed. One amendment required the canal be extended to Bennetts Creek and the authorized stock be increased from $50,000 to $100,000.

The Hamburg Ditch

However, in the early 1850's a few men residing on the western side of Dismal Swamp—including Col. Robert R.

Hill, Samuel Harrell and Timothy Lassiter—cut a twelve-foot wide ditch one-half mile from Holley Grove at a point called Hamburg twelve miles across the swamp to the Dismal Swamp Canal. Tradition states that the terminal was named after the free German city of Hamburg which had engaged in friendly trade relations with the United States after the Revolution.

The ditch proved serviceable in carrying out shingles, lumber and logs and bringing in merchandise for the nearby communities. A store and a bar were operated at the Gates County terminal.

First Railroad Crosses Great Dismal

About 1830 the first railroad was built five miles through Great Dismal between Portsmouth and Suffolk, Virginia by the Portsmouth and Weldon Railroad. The constructors found the undertaking "so formidable a labor, as almost to despair of success." Workmen were plagued by sharp stumps of cut reeds, soft muddy ooze, yellow flies and mosquitoes.

Late in the nineteenth century lumber companies ran rail lines into several parts of the swamp to bring out timber on "bogys" drawn by oxen or mules. The animals were replaced by steam-powered "tram-engines" about 1900.

During the 1920's the first highway through the main part of Great Dismal was cut four miles from Acorn Hill in Gates County to Newland in Pasquotank County. A railroad brought in the sand for construction of the fill which is the roadbed for present U. S. 158.

Before this road only the footbridges laid down by the swamp homesteaders and the trails blazed by the swamp "rats" provided passage through the dark morass.

SWAMPY RIVER SCENE — by Porte Crayon

Haven for the Hunted

CHAPTER XIV

From Borders to Forbidding Recesses

While the borders of the Dismal Swamp may have been a haven for escapists—slaves, outlaws and hermits—during the early colonial period, it was soon before the Revolution, it seems, that they began fleeing into its forbidding recesses.

When the Carolina proprietary was young and sparsely settled the frontier provided a far more suitable hiding place than the fearful morass.

In 1699 Henderson Walker, North Carolina's deputy governor, said so much when he told complaining Virginia "neither are there any runaways here yt we can discover upon diligent enquiry nor shall any such thing be suffered so far as it is our power to prevent it." Then Walker tells of pursuing runaways over the Albemarle Sound as far as Pamlico. This country was most inhospitable to them, for "some of ym died by famine in ye uninhabited part of this government." He expressed the belief that many others seeking sanctuary in Carolina "are lost after ye same or such like manner."

Virginians remained unconvinced of North Carolina's diligence in hunting out runaways. In 1714 Governor Spotswood echoed earlier complaints that both escaped slaves and persons fleeing justice were finding sanctuary within the Carolina border.

In 1728 William Byrd voiced the same opinion. He came upon a family of mulattoes in a wooded area east of Great Dismal and said their "Freedom seem'd a little Doubtful." He recalled the long-established Virginia view "many Slaves Shelter themselves in this Obscure Part of the World" where white neighbors helped to shelter them for cheap labor. He said the Carolina people also had extended "like Indulgence" to debtors and criminals.

By the Revolution there is direct reference to escapists living within the Dismal Swamp. In 1777 Elkanah Watson journeyed from Suffolk to Edenton "near the north border of the Great Dismal Swamp, which at this time was infested by concealed loyalists and runaway slaves." These people, Watson explained, were so desperate they "could not be approached with safety." They had been attacking travelers often and had recently killed a Mr. Williams.

The Tories came from hiding following the Revolution, but they were replaced by increased numbers of runaway slaves. Isaac Weld discovered "wild men" to be living in Dismal Swamp and inferred that escapists had been making it their home for a number of years.

The inaccessible Dismal "has afforded shelter for fugitive Negroes," explained Charles William Janson, an English merchant, in his "The Stranger in America 1793-1806."

Later reports reveal that sanctuaries for the escapists were upon the sand ridges which lay behind deep primeval black gum forests providing a one-to-two-foot-deep water barrier and frightful twilight-like shadows or utter darkness where all things moved in secrecy; within an opening upon the dry quivering floor of the tangled juniper forests to which only the skilled swampman could find his way; or amidst the cane and vine jungles where human trails must have moved about as indistinctly as paths of the wild animals.

The colonial slave generally was an outdoor man and knew the ways of the wilds. It was not impossible for large numbers of escapists to learn to live off the swamp forests and the wildlife with little or no help from without. But there were many escapists who ran to Dismal Swamp for sanctuary without subsistence and came out to rob and commit outrages upon the people. Contemporary newspaper reports tell of repeated instances· of such mischief.

A Runaway Slave Turns Highwayman

Such was the story of Pompey Little—Little, because this heavy-set, full-faced, six-foot-tall Negro fellow had worked upon W. P. Little's "Littleton" plantation in Hertford County's Maney's Neck area.

It was frequently stated in the press—and probably by word of mouth—the Gates County side of the Dismal Swamp had become notorious for harboring runaway slaves and that some of them had turned outlaws.

We can't be certain what Pompey had in mind. But one autumn day in 1815—after smokehouses and barns had been fattened and as nipping cold sent yellow leaves fluttering earthward—Pompey laid aside his plantation tasks and took off eastward across the Chowan River into Gates County.

The robust 30-year-old fellow was greatly valued by his master. When it was learned that Pompey was "committing some depredations on some of the citizens of Gates," Little wrote to John Vann of Winton and told him he did not want the slave prosecuted and that he would "make them (the robbed) compensation for whatever injury he had done."

If Pompey returned to the Little plantation, he didn't abandon his devotion to thievery. Within seven years he seems to have become a notorious outlaw by committing robberies about the Dismal Swamp.

One James W. Langley of Plymouth concluded Pompey's story July 1822, as recorded in the "Portsmouth and Norfolk Herald."

The sun was sinking behind the pine forest as Langley traveled along "a rather solitary road about three miles from any house" and "in Gates County about 36 miles south of Suffolk" when big black Pompey stopped Langley's horse. Langley was somewhat shocked by the suddeness because he had been "leisurely riding along reclining in his chair." This outlaw, estimated at 36 or 37 years of age, certainly was well fed, for he was "remarkably fat in the face." He also went about his business in a professional manner by "brandishing a long two-edged knife" as he approached and his readiness to tell Langley he "lied" when Langley said his trunk contained all his money.

However, Pompey proceeded to remove the trunk, and Langley decided it wise to give him money from his person. He handed the robber a bundle of notes, told him to count them and let him know the amount for he "intended to publish the circumstances as soon as he reached Norfolk." Pompey replied he was "welcome to do so" and he could add "his name was Pomp." But as Pompey dug into the notes Langley withdrew a pistol from his coat and emptied "18 buck shot" into the robber's side. A few blows across the head with the gun completed the job.

Further on his way to Norfolk Langley learned that the night previous "some countrymen, who were returning from a market, had been robbed at the same spot by three runaway negroes. . . ."

Free Negroes Turn Outlaw

A March 11, 1820, Suffolk letter entitled "Murder, Outrage and Robbery" in the "Norfolk Herald" opened the crime story of four free Negroes, who with the aid of other persons, committed "diabolical acts of murder and robbery" in Nansemond County, Virginia, and Gates and Hertford counties, North Carolina.

The night of March 9 Robbert Riddick, a substantial

farmer who lived on the main road from Suffolk to Edenton in Gates County and within sight of the Dismal Swamp near present Corapeake, was shot and killed; and the slaying of the 60-year-old man was "supposed to have been the act of a Negro."

About a week earlier, the letter explained, five masked men had attacked Jethro Pender near Murfreesboro in Hertford County, left him for dead, robbed the house of valuables and took a trunk containing $260 in cash. The robbers implicated four local men — William Liles, Jim Spiers, Bill Rogers and Tom Faircloth, who came very near being hanged — by calling each other by the names of these men in the presence of Pender's granddaughter.

Late the evening of October 27, 1820, reported the "Edenton Gazette," one John W. Perry of Hertford County and another man, "in pursuit of a fiddler in order to have a dance," fell in with Jerry Reed upon a by-path about two and one-half miles from Winton. Perry and Reed argued and Reed shot Perry in the breast with a pistol. Perry died and Reed fled the area. The slayer was described as 28 or 30 years old, yellow, thick-set, five-foot seven. He had a speech impediment and was "quite humble when sober." Later intelligence indicated that Reed had headed for the Dismal Swamp area.

A May 21, 1821, letter in the Edenton Gazette" told of one Jesse Corbell, a mulatto, held in the Suffolk jail for the slaying of Captain Shelton of Nansemond County, who had cofessed that he, Jerry Reed, two other mulattoes, Willis Edge and his son Harvey, and "a certain black man unknown," had beat and robbed Pender. Willis and Harvey Edge were taken up. The boy confessed and supported Corbell's confession.

Corbell was executed June 9, 1821, but Willis Edge was acquitted by a jury in the October term of Chowan Superior Court with "no evidence of the fact appearing against him."

Mulatto Jerry Reed continued in the ranks of wanted men. But before the gallows meted justice to Corbell, says the June 4, 1821, "Edenton Gazette," the prisoner "made a disclosure of the following facts to which he was either accessory or privy:

"That to his knowledge Willis Edge and Jerry Reed stole a negro man named Archer, from John Harrell.

"That Samuel Cotton and Jas. Copeland, the men who apprehended him (Corbell) stole a negro girl belonging to Abram Cross.

"That said Reed and Edge stole a negro boy by the name of Daniel from J. Spaight.

"That said Reed and Edge stole a negro woman from David Sumners.

"That Obed, Copeland and Reed stole a boy that belonged to one Brown, or to the estate of Brown, and sold him in Norfolk.

"That Harvey Edge and Reed stole a boy from Abram Cross, and carried him to Davy Davis, who carried him to Norfolk and sold him.

"That said Edge and Reed stole a boy by the name of Willis.

"That he (Corbell) and H. Edge stole a negro boy named Sampson, from D. Summers.

"That Harvey Edge and his father stole a negro from R. O. Jernigan, and sold him in Currituck County, near Knott's Island, and gave him a bill of sale in the name of Eason."

A Negro Outlaw Gang

A gang of six Negro outlaws was prowling the woods and swamps of Gates and neighboring counties in 1824 and proving a nuisance both to the local inhabitants and travelers.

May that year the "Elizabeth City Star" stated these men had committed a "deadly assault in Gates County" upon an anonymous white traveler of Hertford County.

The "Western Carolinian" of Salisbury spoke of the occurence as an "alarming affair!" The journeyman, himself a slaveholder, was passing through a wooded area when the gang, armed with guns, rushed from a thicket into the road to assault and rob him.

The traveler, being unarmed and outnumbered, dashed into the woods and made his escape.

The gang, it was reported, had been commiting acts of violence and plunder for some time.

Great Dismal Feared as Base for Uprisings

The growing number of runaways to the Dismal Swamp became a source of great apprehension for many miles about. Although these escapists concerned themselves chiefly with maintaining their freedom and obtaining subsistence by stealing and plundering with the incidence of arson and murder, the white populace most feared the swamp being used as a place of assembly from which the Negroes could strike out from their sanctuary and undertake extermination of the white settlers.

The fear rose to near panic during Nat Turner's bloody Southampton County, Virginia, massacre in 1831. Upon learning of the seriousness of the uprising, Major General McDonald ordered out the Chowan County militia and took it into Pasquotank County "as a strategic movement to prevent the use of it (Great Dismal) by the Negroes in the adjoining counties of Virginia, as a place of retreat, and for offensive demonstrations."

Already, North Carolina had set up elaborate and efficient machinery for the capture of runaways and to guard against insurrections. Patrols, "nigger dogs," local posses, and the militia were all available.

Determined action was taken to prevent future insurrections. Within about twenty years after the Southampton incident the largest part of Great Dismal, which lay in North Carolina, had been combed almost completely free of escapists.

The "Nigger Traders"

"Nigger traders" made life a bit more comfortable for runaways to Great Dismal. Small farmers, free Negroes, distillers, and small storekeepers bartered or sold food, drink, firearms and ammunition without asking questions and kept their mouths shut.

The traffic was carried on around the southern borders of the swamp which were sparsely settled with small farmers. Hugh Rice of Sunbury quotes "the old people" as saying large numbers of slaves from the Chowan County plantations sought refuge in this area.

Trade with escapists was more open in the Virginia part of Great Dismal. The shingle industries, utilizing the large juniper forests, worked both runaways and gangs of slaves. These escapists were able to obtain the necessities of life with their labor and seem to have given little trouble. For the most part, they were permitted to live in the fastness of the swamp. When the Civil War gave them freedom some had become so attached to swamp life that they continued to live in it and work for the forest industries.

When Frederick Law Olmsted came to the swamp in the winter of 1854 as a representative of the old "New York Times" the "wild men" mentioned by Weld three-quarters of a century earlier were dying out. In his "A Journey in the Seaboard Slave States in the Years 1853-1854 with Remarks on Their Economy" Olmsted describes graphically the relentless routing of the runaway Negro from the swamp's "back places."

As for the wild people, he stated, "Children were born, bred, lived and died here." However, upon his visit he felt there could be "but few of these 'natives' left."

One informant told him that runaways were shot and often killed; and then added, " 'But some of 'em would rather be shot than be took, sir.' "

Slave-hunting had become an organized business some ten years or more earlier with bounties offered and "nigger-dogs" used to search them from the jungles. A farmer borderer told Olmsted of three or four escapees being shot in a single day.

Training "Nigger-Dogs"

"No particular breed of dogs is needed for hunting Negroes, Olmsted explained. "Blood-hounds, fox-hounds, bull dogs and ours were used, and one white man told me how they were trained for it, as if it were a common or notorious practice. The dogs are shut up when puppies, and never allowed to see a Negro except while training to catch one. A Negro is made to run from them, and they are encouraged to follow him until he gets into a tree, when meat is given them. Afterwards, they learn to follow any particular Negro by scent. . . ."

The lumbering slave was given a pass or "free papers" to enable him to travel about the swamp unmolested by hunters of the runaways. A black man taken without such papers was jailed, advertised and, if not claimed, sold at auction.

A slave informant told Olmsted that the hunters could tell an escapee by sight. " 'Oh, dey looks strange. Skeared like, you know, sir, cause dey hasn't much to eat, and ain't decent like we is."

Longs for Plantation Corn Shucking

Alexander Hunter reported in the October 1895 "Outing" he had a long talk in Suffolk with a slave who had remained "hidden in the swamp for nineteen years, and in all that time had never seen the face of a woman. He said that he had plenty of whisky and tobacco, but what he longed for was a real old plantation corn shucking."

"What a life it must be," remarked Olmsted, "born outlaws; educated self-stealers; trained from infancy to be constantly in dread of the approach of a white man as a thing more fearful than wild-cats or serpents, or even starvation."

In order to live in the swamp, he added, it was necessary for the runaways to steal from the plantations, or to seek help of the slave "shingle-getters," who sometimes hired them but sometimes betrayed them for a price to Negro hunters.

Street Finds Old Huts

Frederick Street stated in the March 1903 "Frank Leslie's Popular Monthly" that he had stumbled on the remains of huts used by runaway slaves near the then "largely over-grown and half obliterated" roads used by the shingle makers. He said that some runaways earned enough money working for the "shingle-getters" to buy their freedom and that some had lived in the wilderness as long as thirty years, depending for food and clothing upon "coons," the most plentiful species of game in the Dismal. In his day criminals were being forced from the swamp by starvation.

Folk Tales of Runaways Going Native

Stories of runaway slaves going native still are a part of local tradition around the southern border of Great Dismal. The tales seem to have been fashioned to amuse and amaze children.

In the 1890's when Hugh Rice of Sunbury was a boy upon the swamp near Acorn Hill "old folks told of slaves escaping and hiding in the swamp where many died."

They built bark cabins upon the swamp ridges, and the lack of guns and ammunition forced them to adopt primitive methods of capturing wildlife. They made bows and arrows and hunted like the Indian, the children were told. They also built log traps and deadfalls to capture game, and they took some fish from small ponds.

Large turtles were to be found in abundance in the wet forests, and they added masts and parched acorns to their diet.

Collie Hawks of Savage, who with his father homesteaded on Little Ridge 1813-18, viewed the remains of what were said to be shacks of runaway slaves and "graves of people who had lived there in olden times."

Old Tom Yeates of Acorn Hill recalls stories of "wild men" as told by Isaac Riddick of Corapeake about 1900. When the runaways remained in the wilderness long enough, Riddick had said, they developed the "swamp scent." This was a wild odor which made wild animals less fearful of them. Eventually they learned to eat anything that a bear could and thus enjoyed an abundance of food. Those who neglected to clothe themselves grew a protective covering of hair over their bodies.

Flood of Abolitionist Literature

In the 1840's when a determined effort was made to rid the swamp of runaway slaves abolitionist literature dramatizing the Negro's persecution flooded the Northern market.

It was in the early stages that Henry Wadsworth Longfellow wrote his emotional poem about the Negro who had escaped to the swampland's shelter and cowered "on the quaking turf of the green morass" in terror at the sound of "bloodhounds' distant bay." Indignantly anti-slavery is:

THE SLAVE IN DISMAL SWAMP

By Henry W. Longfellow

In the dark fens of Dismal Swamp
  The hunted negro lay:
He saw the fire of the midnight camp,
  And heard at times a horse's tramp,
And bloodhounds' distant bay.

Where will-o-wisps and glow worms shine
  In bulrush and brake;
Where waving mosses shroud the pine,
  And the cedar grows and the poisonous vine,
Is spotted like the snake.

Where hardly a human foot could pass
  Or human heart would dare,
On the quaking turf of the green morass
  He crouched in the rank and tangled grass
Like a wild beast in his lair.

A poor old slave, infirm and lame;
  Great scars deformed his face;
On his forehead he bore the brand of shame,
  And the rage that hid his mangled frame
Were the livery of disgrace.

All things about were bright and fair,
  All things were glad and free;
Lithe squirrels darted here and there,
  And wild birds filled the echoing air
With songs of liberty.

On him alone was the doom of pain,
  From the morning of his birth;
On him alone the curse of Cain
  Fell like a flail on the garnered grain,
And struck him to the earth.

Port Crayon's Runaway Slave of Dismal Swamp

In 1856 Porte Crayon wrote in "Harpers New Monthly" of escaped slaves working for the "shingle-getters," and sketched and described one of the refugees:

"About thirty paces from me I saw a gigantic negro, with a tattered blanket wrapped about his shoulders, and a gun in his hand. His head was bare, and he had little other clothing than a pair of ragged breeches and boots. His hair and beard were tipped with gray, and his purely African features were cast in a mould betokening, in the highest degree, strength and energy. The expression of the face was of mingled fear and ferocity, and every movement betrayed a life of habitual caution and watchfulness. He reached forward his iron hand to clear away the briery screen that half concealed him while it interrupted his scrutinizing glance. Fortunately he did not discover me, but presently turned and disappeared."

"Dred" the "Wild Man"

Harriet Beecher Stowe contributed little to the realism of the Dismal Swamp she never visited in her anti-slavery novel "Dred" which appeared in 1856 following the phenomenal success of her "Uncle Tom's Cabin." The runaway hero, a curious combination of an Old Testament prophet and a slave-day Messiah, may have been a "companion of owls" which constantly arouse the swamp from its nocturnal slumber, but it is questionable if there were "dragons" to share his company. Dred was fashioned into a "wild man," so much a creature of the swampland that he moved in freedom through the morasses from the Florida Everglades to the Virginia border and finally met his death at the hands of a slave-hunting posse.

SLAVE OF DISMAL SWAMP—by Porte Crayon

Fictional Hordes of Escapees

"Thousands of Negroes" had found sanctuary in the
Dismal's "vast jungle," wrote John Hamilton Howard in

his 1906 novel, "In the Shadow of the Pines, a Tale of Tidewater Virginia." Once a slave escaped into the Dismal, he said, hope of his recapture was abandoned — a statement of fancy.

But many did escape, as Robert Arnold remembered in 1888 in his "The Dismal Swamp and Lake Drummond. Early Recollections":

> ". . . you could not take up a newspaper published in this part of the State but what you would see several cuts of a negro absconding with a stick on his shoulder and a pack on one end of it, with the following advertisement:
>
> " 'Notice! $500 Reward   Ran away from the subscriber, on the night of June 18th, my negro man, Simon   He may be making his way to the Dismal Swamp. . . .' "

Then Arnold tells of the capture of a runaway:

> "I knew of an instance just before the late war when a gentleman by the name of Augustus Holly, Bertie County, N. C., had a slave to run away, who was known to be a desperate character. He knew he had gone to the Dismal Swamp. And to get him, his master offered a reward of $1,000 for his apprehension, dead or alive. The person who caught him is still living. I saw the Negro when he was brought to Suffolk and lodged in jail. He had on a coat that was impervious to shot, it being thickly wadded with turkey feathers. Small shot were the only kind used to shoot runaway slaves, and it was very seldom the case that any ever penetrated far enough to injure."

The Old Man of Great Dismal

Several years after the Civil War a very old Negro man, gnarled and grey, showed up in the community of

Jonesville (now Corapeake) beside the Dismal Swamp.

He had come back home to pay for an old crime and live out his remaining time. Long years alone in the vast wilderness had grown heavy upon his wearying spirit.

However, to everyone he seemed a stranger, for he bore no resemblance to anyone they had known.

He allowed it had been a mighty long time since he as a slave had fled into the swamp. How long he didn't know exactly, for the years had passed without the counting. He had fled when he killed a white man at the nearby mill-pond in an ownership dispute over a large fish they had caught together with entangled lines.

Old people remembered faintly both the dead man's name and a story their parents had told. But that was a long time past—maybe a hundred years.

The local justice was uninterested in the old man's confession. But after a few more days had passed he told the folks he had to pay for his crime anyway.

They didn't understand.

The slain man's spirit had discovered his return, they were told, and was after him. "I'se boun' to go back to (the loneliness of) dat swamp!"

The old man of Great Dismal was said last seen as he and his walking cane passed slowly along a narrow dusty way which journeyed beside the swamp.

The "Shingle-Getters"

Slaves were employed in Dismal Swamp in the late eighteenth century, first as farm workers for the Dismal Swamp Land Company and then as timber men. Later large numbers also were needed to dig the network of canals and ditches.

A spectacular form of life made the "shingle-getters" a legend.

When Olmsted made his 1854 visit great gangs of

CARTING SHINGLES—by Porte Crayon

slaves, numbering as many as 100, were brought into the swamp. Most of the men were hired from owners living on the outside, at about $100 a year each.

The slaves entered the swamp in February and lived and worked in it ten months. They built their huts on the rare high ground upon an accumulation of shavings from previous workings. Shingles, fashioned by hand, were their chief industry. However, some slaves cut cypress for ship timber or fence rails to be sold on northern markets at seven cents each.

In the swamp the slave enjoyed unusual freedoms. A pass permitted him to roam the swamp in quest of pelts, and he also received a ten-month supply of clothing and provisions. When he was not working he could hunt and fish, drink and eat, play and sleep much as he pleased.

This swamp worker assumed a sense of responsibility. In addition to the profit from his pelts he received two months vacation from work.

One slave told Olmsted he liked the swamp life because he could "mind himself." And Olmsted observed the slave lumberman was "more sprightly and straightforward" than plantation slaves.

Edmund Ruffin wrote in the January 1, 1837 "The Farmers' Register" of the swamp slave's healthy and happy state:

> "Their houses, or shanties are barely wide enough for five or six men to lie in . . . a fire (is) kept up through the night. The roof is sloping . . . and . . . not above four feet from the floor. Of the shavings made in smoothing the singles, (beds are prepared) . . . Yet they live plentifully, and are pleased with their employment—and the main objection to it with their masters, (they being generally slaves,) and the community, is that the laborers have too much leisure time, and of course spend it improperly. Their

> heavy labors for the week are generally finished in five, and often in four days—and then the remainder of the week is spent out of the swamp, and given to idleness . . . About 500 men are thus employed in the whole swamp . . . With all their exposure, the laborers are remarkably healthy, and almost entirely free from the autumnal fevers that so severely scourge all the surrounding country. It is said that no case has yet occurred of a shingle-getter dying of disease in the swamp, nor did my informants know that anyone had been so sick as to require to be brought out."

HORSE CAMP—by Port Crayon

"Horse Camp" and "Nimble-Footed" Mules

Porte Crayon wondered why the "Horse Camp" was a place where mules were kept as well as serving as headquarters for the shingle-makers. This was "a group of picturesque sheds" which provided accomodations for "a number of men and mules."

The "nimble-footed" mule was a marvel of agility in getting over the "rough and unsteady causeway quite rapidly and in understanding Negro lingo. He was "managed entirely by words and gestures, mostly consisting of oaths and kicks."

UPON LAKE DRUMMOND—Virginia Chamber
of Commerce photo

[172]

Marvelous Lake Drummond

CHAPTER XV

The Heart of a Weird Swampland

Lake Drummond—heart of a weird swampland wilderness—is the most marvelous and mysterious part of the Dismal Swamp.

Little wonder. Its brandy-brown water—stained by cypress and juniper roots—carves six square miles from wild jungles and sparkles as a jewel beneath sun-lit and moon-lit skies.

The lake's surface pulsates gently or violently to the silent whisper of the breeze or the harsh-bidding of the storm.

She sits in a crater-like cradle above the floor of the surrounding swamplands, receives no streams but disgorges herself into five rivers.

"She's bottomless," some oldtimers explained, but Frederick Street said later, "There are one or two springs . . . from which the water bubbles up with peculiar purity."

Scraggly time-worn trees and snaggly moss-draped tree stumps shape her "dusky" shores.

She fed upon Indian legends and folk tales of serveral generations, and for many years the milk of fantasy which had flowed from the bard Moore's pen . . . until Porte Crayon arriving at her brink shouted, " 'The Lake!' . . . the dream of my childhood fulfilled . . . neither new nor strange. I had seen it a thousand times in my waking and sleeping dreams . . . the broad expanse of dusky water with its dim circling shores, the same dark leaden waves rolling over its surface and losing themselves silently among the reeds and rushes. Then those gigantic skeletons of cypress that rose so grandly in the foreground, their wild contorted limbs waving with weepers of funereal moss, that hung down even to the water. . . . a picture of desolation—Desolation."

Encompassed in the shrouded vista were places like Jack the Hermit's Camp, the Old Fisherman's Shed, the Stooping Pine, the Three Cypresses, the Forked Gum, the Wharf Log, and entries of five ditches.

In 1838 a roving reporter for the "Southern Literary Messenger" found "a shed of boards much like a cowhouse" in which lived an old fisherman and his family.

Upon the lake another fisherman and his daughter, "a pretty sunburnt girl of fourteen," had their log canoe "well laden with fish."

At the end of Jack's Road—an old "bogy" line running six miles from Corapeake to the lake—was Jack's Camp.

Jack— sometimes called Black Jack, the Hermit—was a fabled character before the middle of the nineteenth century as a swamp devotee who made his living hunting and fishing. A legend says Old Jack's long life was concluded only by conspiracy of the evil swamp spirits. He was deceived by them one cold winter and froze to death.

Before 1803, when Irishman Thomas Moore wrote "The Lake of the Dismal Swamp," Lake Drummond was a vast sheet of water hidden away in the Dismal Swamp wilderness.

An Irishman Visits Great Dismal's Lake

Moore came to Norfolk in the fall of 1803 while serving in a minor colonial post at Bermuda. He may have heard the legend of the Firefly Lady of the Dismal as a guest of Norfolk's British consulate, but some suggest he picked it up at a grog house.

If Robert Arnold and his informant, Uncle Tony, an old Negro intimately familiar with the lake, are to be believed, one morning the dapper Irishman took off for the lake. Uncle Tony was getting his skiff ready to go down a ditch to the lake when " 'a mity nice lookin' man cum up to me an' sed "Buck, ar you de man dat will carry me to de lake of de Dismal Swamp, for which I will pay you one pound?" The gentman talked so putty dat I tole him to git in my skif an' I wood carry him to de Lake.' "

When Uncle Tony stopped at the horse camp " 'to git somfin to eat' " his passenger treated him with a drink of "Irish whiskey" and " 'told me dat his name was Thomas Moore.' "

Uncle Tony professed to be frightened when told by Moore he was going to the lake to write " 'bout a spirit dat is seed dar paddlin' a kunne,' " as told him in Norfolk.

Moore was quite impressed by the lake, said Uncle Tony. " 'He tole me dat he had trabbled an' seen sites, but dat nebber wus so 'stonish befo'; he did not 'spec' to see at de end ob de kunel (canal) sich a putty place, an' dat I wood hear some time what he was gwine tu say 'bout it.' "

Moore's lyrical story of a bereaved lover, who in grief fled to the swamp in pursuit of the shade of his dead sweetheart, entranced London. The lake and the swamp was immortalized.

He prefaced his verses with the inspiring legend: "They speak of a young man who lost his mind upon the death of a girl he loved, and who, suddenly disappearing from his friends, was never afterward heard of. As he had frequently said, in his ravings, that the girl was not dead. but gone to the Dismal Swamp, it is supposed he had wandered into that dreary wilderness, and had died of hunger, or been lost in some of its dreadful morasses."

THE WHITE CANOE—by Porte Crayon

A BALLARD—THE LAKE OF DISMAL SWAMP
By Thomas Moore

They made her a grave too cold and damp
    For a soul so warm and true;
She has gone to the Lake of Dismal Swamp,
Where all night long, by fire-fly lamp,
    She paddles her white canoe.

Her fire-fly lamp I soon shall see,
    Her paddle I soon shall hear;

Long, long, and loving our lives shall be,
I'll hide the maid in a cypress-tree
   When the footsteps of death are near.

Away to the Dismal Swamp he speeds;
   His path was rugged and sore,
Through tangled juniper, beds of reeds,
And many a fen, where the serpent feeds,
   And man never trod before.

And when on the ground he sunk to sleep—
   If slumber his eyelids knew—
He lay where the deadly vine doth weep
Its venomous tear, and nightly steep
   The flesh with blistering dew.

And near him the she-wolf stirred the brake,
   The coppersnake breathed in his ear;
'Til startling, he cries, from his dreams awake,
"Oh! when shall I see the dusky lake,
   And the white canoe of my dear?"

He saw the lake, and a meteor bright
   Quick over its surface played;
"Oh, welcome," he cried, "My dear one's light!"
And the dim shores echoed for many a night
   The name of the death-cold maid.

He hollowed a boat of the birchen bark,
   Which carried him off from the shore;
Far, far, he followed the meteor spark,
The winds were high and the clouds were dark,
   And the boat returned no more.

But oft from the Indian hunter's camp
   This maid and her lover so true,
Are seen, at the hour of midnight damp,
To cross the lake by a fire-fly lamp,
   And paddle their white canoe.

Other Fire-fly Poems Inspired

Moore's Firefly Lady inspired poems which lacked his spark of greatness. In 1851 Howard H. Caldwell heard one sung by some ladies while he visited in Virginia.

He spoke of it as a "strangely wild and striking melody" which told of the grief of an Indian brave who had slain his bride and then went in quest of her spirit in the depths of the swamp. The first stanza as given by Caldwell:

Come to the Lake of the Dismal Swamp,
    I wait in my light canoe,
The pale moonbeams dim my firefly lamp,
    And my drink is the midnight dew."

Caldwell himself sought to explain the murder of the Firefly Lady in his poem "Oliatta" published in 1855, but this muddled work was a total literary failure.

Indian Love Tale

In 1908 Alexander Hunter published in "The Huntsman in the South" an Indian love story, in some ways similar to Moore's

Before the coming of the white man, when Indian lore was rich with stories, a poor Indian warrior and the daughter of his tribe's chief fell deeply in love. The father would not consent to their marriage. But their love was so great they ran away to the fastness of the Dismal Swamp. Here they found perfect happiness and at times they were seen to cross the lake together.

Eventually their days of bliss upon earth drew to an end. After crossing the vast water expanse one day they were never seen alive again.

However, the Great Spirit had been pleased with their high and rare love. To this day he graciously permits them to return to the familiar haunts of their earthly bliss. The lovers are seen to take a midnight canoe trip upon Lake Drummond, then to vanish into heaven, leaving only a meteor spark to mark their path.

The Phantom Fisherwoman

It was not uncommon to see the phantom fisherwoman along the wild southwest shore of Lake Drummond. Some thought her a beneficient deity of the swampland and others an evil spirit who lured lost hunters to their doom in the swamp's depths. When people drew too near she would disappear.

Arnold reported that one gentleman, who had called at lakeside Lake Drummond Hotel, claimed to have seen her five miles across the lake as distinctly as if she had been but a few feet away.

One morning she came from the wilderness "so thick with reeds, bam-boo and rattan, that you could not get three feet from the shore." The beautifuly, finely dressed spectre walked out on a log, baited her hook and cast it into the lake.

She was pointed out to others when she reappeared at the same place and time of day for several days.

Swamp Water With a Kick

Porte Crayon tells of a stranger calling at Lake Drummond Hotel who saw before him in a bottle a liquid he took to be brandy. He cut it with a clear liquid from another bottle. The drink was rather strong and he "kept on watering and drinking until he was entirely drunk and thoroughly perplexed.

" 'Landlord!' " he stammered, " 'come here. This is darn'd queer brandy of yours. The more water I put in the stronger it gets.' "

It was then explained that the brown liquid was swamp water and the clear liquid, whiskey.

Fire Theory of Lake's Origin

One theory contends that shallow saucer-like Lake Drummond was created in prehistoric times by peat fires. Thus the lake would have been a peat bed which was ignited during an extended dry period—perhaps by lightning or an Indian fire.

At other places in the swamp peat formations consist of a brown mass of vegetable matter derived chiefly from juniper which generally ranges from eight to ten feet deep. At times seventy-five to ninety-five per cent of the soil is of organic matter. The greatest depth of the lake is about the same as that of the peat beds.

The ability of peat fires to reshape Dismal Swamp was revealed from 1923 to 1926 when about one-hundred-and-fifty miles were burned over destroying the forests.

Nonetheless, the preferred theory is that Lake Drummond is the remains of a larger pond which has been shrinking since retirement of an ancient sea.

Dismal Swamp Marvels

CHAPTER XVI

The "Green Sea" of Dismal Swamp

Five miles south of Lake Drummond and two miles east of Holley Grove—hidden away in Dismal Swamp—lay the mysterious and novel "Green Sea."

Adventurers returned from the wilderness to tell of its unchanging green surface and its mystery. Here waves rolled tirelessly—gently when there seemed to be no breeze and roared angrily to the bidding of the wind. It seemed possessed with the same phantom-like spirit as the encompassing swamp forest.

Ten to fifteen feet below the surface of the Green Sea could be found fish in small pools and secretive land animals. Here the large "cow" bear piled up grassy heaps as a haven for contented wintertime sleep, the silent-footed wildcat came sneaking through tunnels, and Old Ringtail the coon ventured from the forested swamp in quest of delicate food tidbits.

The Green Sea was one of the first recorded marvels of Dismal Swamp. It was a jungle of evergreen reeds springing from a marsh bottom and towering as lusty canes to simulate the appearance, action and sound of a sea.

In 1728 William Byrd apparently was told of the natural wonder by the local settlers. At the home of Peter Brinkley near present Corapeake in Gates County, North Carolina, Byrd listened carefully to the hardships the dividing line survey party had endured while cutting their

GREEN SEA AFTER ITS BURNING IN 1914— Louis Benton photo

way fifteen miles through Dismal Swamp. Then he wrote in his diary, "There is one remarkable part of the Dismal, lying south of the Line, that has few or no Trees growing on it, but contains a large Tract of tall Reeds. These being green the year round, and waveing with every Wind, have procur'd the name of the Green Sea."

As time and generations passed the mystery of the Green Sea increased in swampside lore. It became the haunt for the bear and the dwelling place for even more dreadful creatures—grotesque and monstrous animals and hideous and evil spirits.

Apparently those early west-side settlers were telling tales quite similar to those Byrd had heard on the swamp's east side where his men were amused with "Idle Stories of Lyons, Panthers and Alligators they were likely to encounter" in the dreadful morass.

Like Paradise Old Fields, a grassy waste upon Jerico Ditch north of Lake Drummond, Green Sea was closely associated in lore with Great Dismal's mysterious lake. Both places were filled with grottos, old timers said, and it was supposed the fairies and evil spirits came to them by subterranean passages.

The Green Sea waved on in fact until 1914 when during an extended dry period a fire reduced the fabled place to black cane stubbles and charred skeletons of gallberry bushes.

At that time Tobe Daniels, who lived beside the Dismal at Orapeake Swamp, was its owner. He cut a ditch through the marsh to Hamburg Ditch, drained it, and the Green Sea never returned. A lush growth of grass replaced the reeds, and upon this Daniels grazed large herds of cattle.

The old Green Sea became the Old Light as an opening in the swamp or the Big Marsh on Hamburg Ditch where a growth of trees, chiefly juniper and pine, is seeking to replace the grass.

Beginning of a Dismal Swamp River

The Pasquotank, one of Dismal Swamp's seven rivers, rises in a manner as mysterious as the swamp itself.

First there are endless pools of black slimy water groping about the bottle-bottomed cypress and black gum trees, with no apparent source or destination.

But somewhere in the morass little streams, like The Moccasin Track, wind tediously through thicket tangles until they eventually find another one like the Horseshoe. A few of these and there is a little branch, which grows into a deep and narrow river, then quits winding aimlessly and widens purposefully—Majestically.

Local lore says for more than two hundred years no two people could be found who would agree where the Pasquotank River ended and the tricklets began. The State Supreme Court settled the matter about 1917 to hush complaints of two covetous lumber companies.

The headwaters, the story continues, were established at a point north of Newland where a black gum tree bore axe marks. Rufus Hewitt of Newland says a local resident had paddled a row boat up the stream as far as he could go, stepped ashore and marked the tree as the head of the river. Today both a concrete marker and a railroad marker stand there. Richmond Cedar Works erected the concrete marker as its line, and Roper Lumber Company buried a section from one of its old "bogy" rails to mark the same spot.

Two Dividing Lines of "Four-Mile Desart"

Until about 1900 Pasquotank and Perquimans counties, both formed in 1670, either had a mythical dividing line or two dividing lines in the southeast branch of Dismal Swamp.

They were a long time in running lines in this wild

place which local people still know as the "Four-Mile Desart." When sheer estimation was no longer satisfactory each county ran its own line.

This resulted in two lines, about 500 feet apart, says local tradition. However, no one seemed to mind the difference until lumber companies grew interested in removing the timber. The counties then declared the unclaimed area a no-man's-land until a joint survey established ownership.

The Two Bear Types of Dismal Swamp

Fact or fancy—there are two kinds of bears in Dismal Swamp. They are known both to literature and lore as the little "hog" bear and the large "cow" bear.

How do they differ?

In size, color and some habits.

Anywhere around Great Dismal today one can learn that the "hog" bear is the small satin-black bear which grows large enough to manage a hog with ease—thus his name. He is a frequent visitor to the borders of the swamp.

The "cow" bear wears a deep brown coat and has a large light brown or white spot beneath his throat. He has been known to exceed eight hundred pounds, and the larger ones are so powerful they can manage a cow with ease. His normal habitat is the deep and wild parts of the swamp, and he is rarely seen and taken.

The "cow" bear is artful in capturing a cow, especially the ferocious wild one, explains D. E. Darnec, retired Gates County game protector. The bear climbs a tree beside a cow path and drops from it onto her back. As the cow runs and tries to disengage him he gnaws into the tendon in the back of her neck. When this has been severed her head falls and she can run no further.

A domesticated cow runs for the hill, and the wild cow goes for the swamp ridge where she lives. Some bears

brought from the swamp by cows have been shot and killed. At Acorn Hill, says Hugh Rice, a work steer was
attacked and his angered farmer-owner slew the bear with
a fence rail.

The bear stops the cow whenever and as soon as possible, according to tradition; and Thurmond Lassiter says if
she passes near a tree, he will grab it with one arm. His
strength usually exceeds hers, and in such event she can
only run in circles about the tree.

The "hog" bear is not so easily frightened as his large
brother. Swamp lore claims he frequented the shanties
of the lumber company workers in quest of garbage and
at times Negroes fed him from their dinner pails. It was
not uncommon for the bear to peep curiously through
the shanty windows and sometimes scratch on the doors.

Once Captain H. B. Winslow was with a party of men
who cut a bee tree on Lake Drummond. "Before we had
gotten out of sight we saw several bears loping towards
the tree."

The Long Bear Fence

A zig zag rail fence, constructed before the memory of
today's older people, once stretched about eleven miles
beside the old Indian trail and along the western border
of Great Dismal Swamp from Green Fork near the southern extremity of the swamp to the Corapeake community
on the Virginia border.

Although it looked like the ordinary rail fences which
farmers used to keep roving livestock from their fields, it
became one of the better known landmarks of the nineteenth century.

Everyone knew a bear could go over the fence where-
ver he pleased "without knocking off the top rail." Yet it
was called The Long Bear Fence.

The fence was actually a giant trap to capture "the

smartest creature" of Dismal Swamp whose ravenous appetite drove him to the borders to feast upon cow's and swine's flesh when his natural food grew in short supply. He had no difficulty returning safely from his foray if the animal he attacked had wandered into the swamp wilderness too far for its cries to be heard by its owner.

Thus the farmers decided to make the bear come onto the highland near their dwellings for his prey, and the fence went up to prevent the open range livestock from wandering into the swamp.

The fence, says Hugh Rice after tradition, was built "by everyone who had a piece of property on the swamp." The people got together and mauled pine and juniper rails, and late each winter more rails were made to keep the fence in repair.

Each time the cry of an attacked animal was heard the ox horn called out the neighbors with guns and dogs. Usually the bear was slain.

Wild Cattle and "Cow Horn" Deer

Until recent years wild cattle, hogs and goats were to be found in Dismal Swamp; and the ferocity of the cattle made them extremely dangerous to the hunter.

These small active cattle were descended from domestics which had strayed from the fields and taken up abode in the swamp. In 1903 Frederick Street said it was impossible to track these cattle through cane brakes. It was customary for swamp guides to clear out "a number of old mule paths" and have the hunters to await beside them until the cattle were driven by much like deer.

A few years ago one wild cattle hunter was chased up a tree near Lake Drummond by a maddened bull. Fortunately he took his gun up with him.

The "cow horn deer," which is captured about the swamp, has made an imprint on local lore. This deer is similar to the point buck in size and color, but his pointless horns curve back like those of a cow—thus his name.

Some borders contend that this deer is a cross with the wild goat; also there is a theory his oddity comes from a food deficiency.

"Old Tom's" Strange Swamp Creature

Old Tom Yeates was born beside Dismal Swamp August 26, 1881, and has lived on and in it the better measure of a century. His present home is one-half mile west of it in the Gates County community of Acorn Hill.

Like most old swampers, Old Tom delights in story telling. As he reels off an amazing number of yarns it becomes clear that he is a recording of lore received from old people who lived beside Dismal Swamp from Sandy Cross to Corapeake.

One of his oldest yarns came from "Old Man Isaac Riddick" of Corapeake as told about 1900, and is as wild as the swamp wilderness.

One day a man came running from the swamp so frightened and upset that it took him some time to stammer that he had been chased out by a frightful creature.

It wasn't a bear, the more likely creature, he insisted, although hair covered its body and it walked on its hind feet.

It wasn't a panther cat; but it did scream like one.

Next day a group of men armed themselves heavily and went into the swamp wilderness with dogs. The creature was taken alive from a tree, brought out and caged.

Everyone—plain country folks and swampers alike—shook their heads in wonder. It wasn't quite like anything that anyone had ever seen in or about the swamp.

People remembered strange old stories strikingly similar to the capture of this creature. Could they be true? Were there wild people in unexplored parts of the wilderness?

Indeed, they were not sheer fancy! All doubt was routed when the creature's hair was shorn off.

Then—an almost forgotten story, which had created widespread interest a quarter of a century earier, was recalled.

A man and his wife had lived on the swamp hill. The man obtained their living from the swamp, and each evening as he came home his woman walked into it apiece to meet him. Each time he would take their baby daughter from her arms and walk the child to their cabin.

At twilight one day the baby was handed to a dim form upon the pathway. Hairy arms received her and without uttering a sound and without a whimper from the child the form disappeared into the wilderness. A search for the lost child was fruitless.

Now, in the cage surely was the grown-up baby who had been raised by a mother bear.

As in the old tales—the child soon adopted the wild smell of the swamp and was never feared or molested by other swamp creatures. The mother bear nursed her as her own cub and taught her to eat the natural foods of the swamp.

"What ever happened to her?"

Old Tom pondered. "Both her parents were dead, and I suppose there was nothing else to do but to turn her over to an animal show."

"Old Joe" the Hermit's Companion

Old Tom Yeates' favorite story is about Joe Harrell, who may have lived almost a century as a swamp hermit not far from Corapeake.

Old Tom heard his story from Old Joe's own lips about forty years ago. Interesting enough on its own, amazingly it reveals survival of "Lyon" lore as observed by William Byrd two centuries earlier.

Old Tom didn't ask old Joe how long he had lived in

the swamp, but afterwards folks claimed he was born in there. He must have been well past eighty when Old Tom knew him, and by then he seemed to be a natural fixture of the wilderness.

Old Joe's shack was built permanently as swamp shacks go. It was a small cabin of juniper poles which had both a floor and one end daubed with mud like a stick chimney for his fires. Yet only a small opening in the roof let out smoke and breathed lightning-bug-like sparks into the inky swamp nights.

He also enjoyed the luxury of an old cot, a few pots and pans, and a ragged rug on his floor.

Old Joe lived off the swamp as a hunter and trapper, and he made occasional visits to Corapeake for grub and ammunition in exchange for his pelts.

Here the people learned of Old Joe's love for the swamp and its wild creatures. Surely he had friends; he had cultivated the comradeship of all the animals in the vicinity of his cabin. They were unafraid of him, and he spoke of them as "my neighbors." He traveled to distant parts of the swamp to take his game.

Once a large bear began coming to Old Joe's cabin to pick up his garbage, first at night and then by day. Old Joe tossed him additional food and brought him near enough to pat his head. Day by day their friendship grew, and eventually the bear frequented the cabin as much as Old Joe. As Old Joe rested upon his cot the bear took his place in a corner of the cabin. If the bear arrived late at night, he'd scratch on the door until Old Joe let him in.

After a long comradeship—one night a weird cry moved through the swamp forest to the vicinity of Old Joe's cabin. The bear wheeled about uneasily and then scratched on the door to be let out.

Moments later savage snarls and cries awakened the swamp's death-like darkness and kept it awake most of the night.

At light Old Joe found the mangled bodies of the bear and lion lying together beside the pathway. Only then—after long years in the wilderness—did Old Joe know the value of friendship. The bear had sacrificed his life in his defence.

Old Johnnie Culpepper's "Bear Latin"

Old Johnnie Culpepper of Queen's Ridge claimed to be a descendant of Lord Culpepper, who years ago gave his name to Culpeper Island.

Yet Old Johnnie's acquaintances were more impressed with his skill at hunting, fishing, trapping and guiding people about the swamp. More than that, as a teller of tall tales about Dismal Swamp.

His understanding of the swamp was such that he could talk "bear Latin," which he told Margaret Davis in 1934 he had put to use once when he caught a bear in a log trap.

"Gumpty, sifty, Gumpty, sifty, goggle claw," the bear grumbled out at his captor.

"Sniffle giffle, Sniffle gi; hold fast to your timber tie," knowing Old Johnnie gibbered back.

The bear understood, but Old Johnny never found good reason to interpret his "bear Latin" for benefit of highlanders.

Slaying of Julius Casear's Deer

Visiting highlanders regarded many of old Johnnie's stories as tall tales, continued Miss Davis. Nonetheless, he delighted in reeling off swamp sagas. She took particular note of one about his slaying of Julius Caesar's deer.

How did he know it was Julius Caesar's deer? A strap about his neck bore this poem:

"When Julius Caesar here did reign,
    About my neck he hung this chain;
And whosoever me shall take,
    Save me for Julius Caesar's sake."

"Ol' Aunt Hannah," Caretaker at "Glencoe"

"Amid the rich glooms and shadows of beautiful, abandoned Glencoe—oldest, most storied home-site of the Wallace holdings," says Margaret Davis, "lives the ancient Negress known as 'Ol' Aunt Hannah.' She is pushing ninety now, a tiny shrivelled figure. White-aproned and neat, a hat firmly on her head, a pipe still more firmly between her teeth, a string of blue-grass 'witch-beads' around her neck to ward off harm, she leaves 'Glencoe' daily to the John Wallace home to 'wash dishes for Miss Mildred,' as she calls Mrs. Wallace. By night, according to local tradition, 'Ol' Aunt Hannah' walks abroad quite fearlessly anywhere in the swamp unmolested by its ghosts and 'hants.' Midwife and nurse and prophetess accorded fame in her own country is 'Ol' Aunt Hannah. Many a night-wanderer in the swamp has spied her, a lantern balanced on her head, a basket laden with gifts of cream or eggs, bound for some remote house on an errand of mercy."

"Ol' Nicholas Cherry" of "Cross-roads Store"

" 'Ol' Nicholas Cherry,' " says Margaret Davis, "was a storekeeper in the (Dismal) swamp. He used to sit peacefully beside his tiny stove all day, spitting widely, infallibly and afar. To would-be purchasers he was wont to remark placidly and often, 'My son Nicholas will be here in a few minutes and if he has a mind to wait on you he can do it. I haven't got a mind to get up for five cents myself!' "

Dismal Swamp Mysteries

CHAPTER XVII

Legend of Buried Gold

One legend seeks to explain why occasionally within and about Great Dismal Swamp are heard a confusion of strange voices—eerie echoes of voices that know no habitation—French voices sounding merrily in the evening, laughing and calling to each other—voices of French sailors searching for lost treasure through dark nights.

Margaret Davis reported the legend she had found at the ancient village of Deep Creek, northern terminal of the Dismal Swamp Canal, in the April 1934 "South Atlantic Quarterly."

There's buried gold in the area. No one knows where, for the mystery which helps to enshroud it arises from the seventeenth century . . . when French and English adventurers were on none too friendly terms.

A French warship, loaded with money to pay French soldiers in America, was blown from her course upon the Atlantic by a raging northeaster. She dared into Hampton Roads haven and then into more secretive Elizabeth River.

Unfortunately, she was spied by a British man-of-war, lying hard by the chief avenue to the Virginia Colony. The waship's sails went up into the gale to give the unhappy Frenchmen chase. The same lusty wind sped the French vessel up the Southern Branch of Elizabeth River—all too hurriedly. There was no hoped-for egress to take her again onto the stormy sea—only narrower and narrower waters choked more and more by dense forests.

At the mouth of Deep Creek the French vessel foundered, but she was to be no prize of the hated British. She was put to the torch; fire stripped her sails and gutted her vitals as the Frenchmen sped away up Deep Creek in small boats loaded with the gold.

The English, well aware they had the Frenchmen quarried, gave hot pursuit. Still they were denied the gold, for somewhere along the shores or beneath the waters of Deep Creek the Frenchmen hid the treasure . . . then on and on into the Great Dismal's morass they fled.

Finally, overtaken by the British sailors, they "stood and fought as brave subjects of his Christian majesty, the King of France," and died.

The swamp-dwelling Culpepper family, which claimed lineage from Virginia's distinguished Lord Culpepper, have now and then heard voices in the swamp which can be none other than conversing spirits of the lost Frenchmen.

Schooner of the Dismal Swamp

South of U. S. 158, not far from the Gates County community of Acorn Hill and deep in Dismal Swamp the wet black gum forest once gave way to a big opening which local people called The Light Streak. It spread forth about one mile in each direction as a tangle of grass and cattails.

The Light Streak came from the misty past as one of Dismal Swamp's many places of mystery. It contained enough of the hazards of the wilderness to be the subject of folk stories and to challenge adventuresome young people.

Trees felled by the shingle makers as footbridges and footpaths led more than a mile into the wilderness to the opening and provided a safe trail for visitors.

Yet there were other hazards—swamp cats and large snakes. And the old people pointed shaking fingers as they warned the place also was one of the favorite haunts of the large bear.

Yet with each warning the appetite of the adventuresome youth was sharpened with stories of the mystery ship whose carcass was lying concealed near the center of the great waste.

Only the imagination of the story teller could explain when and how the two-master schooner found its way through the forest almost a score of miles from navigable water.

It came upon a flood . . . was a stranded phantom the like of which had been seen upon the Albemarle Sound . . . came by some channel since closed . . .

The hulk, by whatever means, was there. Hugh Rice, a boy of ten in 1888, was told by his mother that she, her brothers and other young people of the swampside community during her girlhood had visited the derelict and extracted copper nails from her timbers.

As a young man Rice himself came upon the old hulk. The timbers appeared to be very old and resistant to decay, he says. The wood was of fine grain, dark color and unlike any known to the people of the area. The hull had been sheathed in part with copper.

Major W. E. MacClenny of Suffolk, Virginia, reported that the hulk of a large ship was found "near the very center of the Dismal Swamp" and cut in two upon construction of a canal to supply water to Portsmouth. This hulk led to conjecture the swamp onetime was an inland sea.

The Bear Cypress Tree Mystery

The mystery of amassing of bear skeletons beneath the Bear Cypress of the Dismal Swamp as if it were the chosen place for death of countless bears is thought to have been solved . . . or almost so.

Thurmond Lassiter, who spent his boyhood at the old Arnold Place two miles south of Holley Grove, says the tree stands a mile or more eastward in the swamp jungle.

Local tradition had explained that for several generations the infrequent visitor or hunter who came upon the tree observed fresh bear skeletons. Thus as the years accumulated so did the bear skeletons—until the swamp borderers grew curious and began offering a variety of explanations.

Early in the twentieth century, Lassiter's father explained, one Mayward Raby, a swamp guide and surveyor, led two timber prospectors by the tree. The men saw a dead bear lying in the mass of bones, his four feet stretched out and a tall cypress knee impaling his stomach.

Raby recited the traditional stories, but the men made their own observations. The mystery was sent in reluctant retreat.

The large lower limb of the tree reached almost straight out from about sixty feet up. Then far out near its end honey bees were flying to and from a hollow.

It was concluded that for a long number of years the bear had climbed the tree in quest of honey and going out onto the limb required all his climbing skill and use of all four feet.

The task was a precarious one at best. Sometimes the bear got down safely and sometimes he did not.

Once upon the limb the bear had to use one paw to extract the honey. Sometimes when the angered bees swarmed about his eyes and ears a second paw came from the limb to sweep them away. Each time that Bruin reacted so thougthlessly down he swang with his great weight unlatching his hind feet.

A bed of tall cypress knees rose from the soft swamp bottom to receive him. They were the death trap the old tree had made unintentionally for honey-thieving bears.

UNCLE ALICK—by Porte Crayon

Uncle Alick's Climbing Mule

Uncle Alick, "a reverend gentleman of color" who lived near old Booneville upon the Dismal Swamp between Corapeake and Suffolk was certain he owned a mule which could ascend and descend trees.

When Porte Crayon came calling at his home midway the past century he was "a zealous minister of the Gospel" who had been "a pretty extensive sinner in his time."

When Robert Arnold wrote of him in 1888 he was a personage of legendary proportions. He also had a mule which in one way none other equaled.

Some people said the mule had belonged to Nat Turner, leader of the 1831 Southampton County massacre. Yet that wasn't the mule's greatest merit, as the "gospel truth" from "steel-trap-sharp" Uncle Alick himself attested.

Often Uncle Alick went down into Dismal Swamp and cut long paths through the tall reeds in quest of bee trees. So did Uncle Alick's mule, for his own keep on the evergreen reeds.

One day Uncle Alick paused beneath a tall swamp tree and looked up in wonder. All the miracles weren't between the dogged ears of his Bible. His mule was perching high upon a limb of the tree.

Uncle Alick hadn't led him up there and he wasn't leading him down. He hunched his humped shoulders indifferently and wended his way from the swamp to his cabin.

Next morning the mule was home braying at the crow of the rooser—as usual.

The Gibberish-Speaking Hermit

One of the stranger of many Dismal Swamp hermits was reported on by the Albany, New York, "Knickerbocker Press" January 29, 1911.

His home was quaint—sitting in a small opening in the

underbrush reached by a circuitous path. Several poles implanted in the ground supported a coffin-like structure enclosed on three sides but open to the south. Scraps of tin partly shut out the sky.

Long grey hair streamed from the man's unshorn face, and his draping clothing was a marvel of patchwork. His clear friendly voice was unintelligible gibberish.

December 3, 1912, the Norfolk "Virginian Pilot" cleared the mystery in part. The hermit was no wild man. Instead, an Italian immigrant who had sought the Dismal's wilds for an undisclosed reason. This the Norfolk Italian Consul had learned upon a visit to him in 1908.

Varied Witch Lore of Dismal Swamp

Nowhere does witch lore seem so varied as within and about Dismal Swamp. It has been adapted both to swamp and highland situations.

Here, as elsewere, the witch delights in harassing the hunter, usually leads his dogs on a wild chase in the morass for mischief and exhausts them in the difficult terrain.

Some men, like Zanie Daniels of Corapeake, mortally wounded the witch with silver shot. One witch stands as an eerie-looking stump beside Lake Drummond because of one scheming hunter. Once when hard pressed by his dogs she changed herself into the stump. The hunter had brought along an Indian guide possessed with the devil who used his wizardry to fix her in that form.

Sometimes, says the swampsiders, the witch takes the form of a jack-o'-lantern or will-o'-the-wisp and lures the lost stranger in the delusion that a cabin's light awaits him ahead.

Along the southwestern border of the swamp the witch became quite aggressive and in the form of the jack-o'-lantern shot fire arrows at the hapless night traveler.

At Corapeake an old woman who lived beside the swamp would turn herself into a white doe and gather field peas from the fields of her neighbors. Thus, she thought, no one would discover her identity.

Often the witches sought out the deep recesses of Great Dismal on dark nights. Here they delighted in listening to their own shrieking echoes and found comfort in the companionship of restless lost spirits.

At Sandy Cross, in the dark of the moon or on drizzly nights, footsteps of "Big Ditch Mariah," the Indian witch and conjure, could be heard upon lonely swampside pathways. Yet she had no light to guide her mortal way. At such times she was on her way to lay an evil spell.

Timid Ronnie of Sandy Cross

Timid Ronnie Stallings—one night late in the nineteenth century—was timid no more. To his misfortune.

He had spent many nocturnal hours reveling over the cup with the good fellows at Elvy Russel's bar and store at Sandy Cross.

The midnight hour had come and gone before Ronnie and a companion wended their way happily homeward along a pathway that took them near the dangerous border of Dismal Swamp.

Suddenly, "A light!" cried Ronnie.

"A jack-o'-lantern," explained his companion.

"I'm going to catch it!" returned Ronnie as if possessed.

"No—no—no!"

Yet Ronnie plunged like a daredevil towards the thicket and the fireball.

Suddenly the light formed and flew as a flaming arrow towards Ronnie. There came a flash—a peal like a lightning bast—a yellow smoke. Ronnie's companion fled shrieking, terror-stricken.

Next morning he pointed out the spot. Only the prints of poor Ronnie's footsteps were left in the sand.

Dismal Swampside Humor

CHAPTER XVIII

A Smart Bear of Dismal Swamp

"Folks had themselves a time in that old swamp" after it became notorious for its witches, phantoms and wonders, drawled Captain H. B. Winslow of Corapeake who has spent the greater part of his sixty-eight years in Dismal Swamp.

Many an imaginative story trickled matter of-fact from his lips as he sat screened from a pale sultry sun at the knuckled feet of a large tree sprawling over a large part of his back yard.

Then— "you know . . . the bear . . . he's the smartest creature in the swamp." A fact all Dismal people know— yet for those who doubted there was the story as told by one Richard Brinkley, an old hunter and trapper who lived at red clay "Gold Mine Field" upon the Dismal near Orapeake Swamp.

Brinkley was a man who never lacked an attentive audience as he relaxed with the whittlers and wide-eyed youngsters. Yarns fell from his lips as naturally as fluttering leaves before autumn's silent flail.

A monument to his wit was the trapping of a smart "cow" bear. This large fellow was leaving huge tracks and other signs in the swamp back of the Green Sea. So Brinkley built a log trap of juniper poles. He used honey instead of a cow's head for bait, and dabbed bits of it upon the leaves of the tangles to make sure the wind would lay down a distinct trail to his trap.

Dark had fallen when Brinkley arrived home and discovered that in his preoccupation he had left his shotgun standing beside a tree near the trap. It would have to wait until morning; going back into that place at night unarmed was beyond question.

Early next morning a large brown bear had visited the trap when Brinkley came whistling happily along the path. Brinkley stopped suddenly, froze in shock for a moment. Was it possible?

The bear had completed his robbery without getting trapped and seated himself in front of the enclosure . . . "and he had my gun lying across his lap!"

"Did he point it at you?"

"Sure he did; but I shot the hell out of there!"

Great Dismal's Turtle Rider

Many of the more perplexing mysteries of Dismal Swamp were said to have been understood only by the swamp dwellers. Among these were the homesteaders—a hardy set of outdoor-loving and hermit-like people who went into the swamp during the late nineteenth and early twentieth centuries, blazed upon the trees enclosures about their desired holdings, and erected small juniper-pole cabins within.

One homesteader—noted for his devotion to hunting, fishing and exercising his wit upon appreciative cronies—planted his cabin a few miles east of Holley Grove beside so dense a juniper forest that only the owls talked to him by night and the bears came tapping at his door begging for food scraps.

It was necessary for the homesteaders to live in the swamp five years—endure the damp chill of winter and the breathless sultriness of summer. This swamper crept about the swamp with the instinct of its wild creatures, came out to the little store at Holley Grove to bring wonderful tales and returned with provisions.

One day at Holley Grove the homesteader was lamenting the difficult and tiresome trail to his cabin. The conversation quickly turned to the mammoth turtles surviving the centuries in the wilderness sanctuary.

The homesteader cued. "Sometimes when I'm feeling downright poorly," he dragged complainingly, "I jes' gits on de back of one of 'em 'turkles,' and he brings me out."

The homesteader? "Lying" Sam Jones, says Louis Benton.

"My God . . . Didn't We Have a Tussle!"

At Acorn Hill Frunie Pierce, son of a Dismal Swamp homesteader, recited several stories enjoyed by the old-timers of the swampside.

He was at his best with the one about an old man and old woman who lived upon a small farm in a small house beside the big swamp.

One morning as the old woman was cooking breakfast a bear came lumbering from the nearby thicket and headed for the cookroom door. The up-and-about old man saw the bear first and scampered cat-like onto the joists of the unceiled kitchen crying, "Bar the door Margaret, bar the door . . . Jesus Christ, that bear is coming in!"

The old woman picked up the yard broom, beat the critter and sent him loping back into the swamp.

"My God, Margaret, didn't we have a tussle!" bristled the old man as he came down from the joists.

"Wheat Farmer" Upon Great Dismal

People liked to laugh at the foibles of others — especially at the Yankees following the Civil War. In one story:

A Yankee who had come south and purchased a large

farm beside the Dismal Swamp near Corapeake couldn't understand why it wouldn't grow wheat and reap him profits like those enjoyed by mid-western farmers.

Surely it was not because he had bought the farm dirt cheap immediately after the Civil War.

A few years earlier "wheat" was growing shoulder-high on the farm. He had seen it while passing through as an Union officer. Its rankness stuck in his memory, and after the war he returned with ambitious plans.

He carried his first season's failure to his neighbors, and they helped him with an explanation, says Shirley C. Baines.

"Beautiful wheat was growing there back in '64," he told them.

"Oh, that wasn't wheat you saw; that was only broom straw."

It was then explained the farm had gone uncultivated after the slave laborers ran away.

Edward Freeman then became the farm's new owner—at a bargain. He made it into one of the best cotton, corn and peanut producers west of Dismal Swamp.

The Rheumatic and the Bear

Sometimes plots of widely circulated storeies were adapted to the Dismal Swamp scene. All about the borders can be found the one about the Lord and the Devil counting out saints and sinners for their respective rewards.

An old hunter living beside Dismal Swamp had been afflicted with rhematism for several years and had to sit at home day after day longing for the enjoyment of the coon hunt.

However, he had two sons who liked the sport as well as he ever did, and one night he begged them to carry him with them.

"Dad, you know that's impossible; you haven't walked in ten years," he was told.

"Well, roll me (in my wheel chair) down back of the field so I can hear the dogs on the trail."

As requested the old man was left beside the swamp beneath a persimmon tree. The dogs began to make delightful music on old Ringtail's trail as a bear came backing down the persimmon tree.

After the hunt the sons found the empty wheel chair and bear tracks. At least their father had died happy, they consoled themselves, as they rushed to the house to tell the sad news.

To their surprise the old man was safely home waiting for their return—having outrun the bear.

A Dismal Swamp Rescue

During the Civil War a group of Partisan Rangers passed through a swampside community to gather up conscription evaders, and one "buffalo" fled into Dismal Swamp to hide.

However, among the rangers were swampers, and the evader knew he could not use an ordinary hiding place.

Fortunately, not far from his home was a large cypress with a large enough opening about twenty feet up. He scaled the large tree with his spurs and slipped through the hole into its hollow.

Unfortunately, the hollow was larger than the man had estimated and he fell to the bottom amidst two cub bears. A chain of difficulties began. He failed in several attempts to climb out, and he had to box the cubs for a long spell to convince them he wasn't another piece of meat from their mother. By the time he relaxed and began to worry, "How am I going to get out of here?" a bloody piece of meat came tumbling on top of him. A bulky form shut out the overhead light, and the mother bear was heard backing down the hollow.

Fortunately, the man had snatched up a butcher knife in his flight through the kitchen. When the bear came within reach he grabbed her by the tail and jabber her with the knife. Frantically, she clawed out the hollow of the tree sending dead wood flying as she elevated the imprisoned man to the opening and freedom.

A Dismal Swamp Snake Tale

Dismal Swamp snakes, in their protected habitat, understandably may have grown quite large and numerous. However, some snake tales emenating from it seem just such.

Robert Arnold says he was told by a hunter that he once saw "snakes coming from every direction, and quite near him he saw a lump of them that looked to be as large as a barrel." At first the interwoven mass was estimated to contain five hundred. The hunter stepped backward and fired both barrels of his gun at the lump. After they had untangled themselves he counted 150 dead and as many more wounded.

Appropriately, one matched the length of his tale — twenty-three feet.

PART 5

Battle With the Witches

CHAPTER XIX

Colonial Hysteria

Witchcraft hysteria, having spread southward from New England late in the seventeenth century, was a popular madness in North Carolina and Virginia as the first wave of settlers spread over the pocosin-pocked No-Man's-Land upon the Virginia border.

Apparently the prevalent beliefs of the time became firmly rooted upon the frontier, for two centuries later among small segments of the people they were essentially the same, except without the hysteria.

In 1900 the Hall area alone had no less than four old women reputed to be witches; and the prevailing lore gave evidence the devil had kept the witches and his other tributary spirits busy for a long time.

Not long after the witchcraft delusion broke out in Salem, Massachussetts, in 1692, it also is observed in North Carolina. Boston merchants had established commercial ties here, and their small sailing craft apparently promoted social intercourse as well as trade.

Some of the settlers came directly from England, Scotland and Ireland to swell the tide from Virginia. Together they provided an ample supply of witch stories as well as those about fairies, ghosts and ghouls.

Soon belief that supernatural devices were being used

BURNING OF A WITCH

to inflict harm on people had become so prevalent that in North Carolina witchcraft was specifically named among the enumerated offences in the commission granted to justices of the peace, into which they were to inquire, and over which they had jurisdiction.

A 1679 act, preserved in Perquimans County, empowered the justices "To enquire of the good men of the precinct, by whom the truth may be known, of all felonies, witchcraft, enchantments, soceries, magic arts, trespasses, forestallings, regratings and extortions whatever."

In 1697 one Susannah Evans "of the precinct of Curratuck in the county of Albemarle" was indicted for the practice of witchcraft and brought before the Court of Oyer and Terminer. It was charged that Susannah, "not having the fear of God before her eyes, but being led by the instigation of the devil, did, on or about the twenty-fifth day of July last past, the body of Deborah Bouthier, being then in the peace of our sovereign lady the queen, devilishly and maliciously bewitch, and by assistance of the devil, afflict, with mortal pains, the body of the said Deborah Bourthier, whereby the said Deborah departed this life. And also did diabolically and maliciously bewitch several other of her majesty's liege subjects . . ." The grand jury ruled "Ignoramus," thus dismissing the charges.

Tradition has claimed that at least two witches were executed and a third one sentenced to death in North Carolina.

Lawson states that the only capital punishments he had heard of as ever inflicted in the province were of a Turk for murder and an old woman for witchcraft which were "acted many years before I knew the place."

In 1877 John Wheeler Moore states, "The spot is yet pointed out at St. Johns where a hapless Indian woman was said to have been burnt for witchcraft" under the 1679 act.

Return of the London Witch

About 1900 while calling on a family near Winton, a Hall woman herb doctor told of an old woman sentenced to death for witchcraft.

This witch had come directly from England, married and settled with her husband on a sand ridge in the depths of the Chowan River pocosin.

The swamp island upon which their home was built was so small they had difficulty raising enough corn and sweet potatoes to go with the wild fruits they gathered and the wild animals and fish they trapped and caught.

They had little company, for the only way to their place was a footbridge made of trees felled end to end across a wide, mucky and watery swamp.

Eventually their children grew up and moved away and the neighbors were asked to help "lay-away" the husband.

The corpse had a dreadful look—face set with deeply drawn lines and the eyes, which could not be made to close, seemed still alive with fear.

The widow chose to become a hermit rather than move from her swamp island. She seemed so happy in her lonely wilderness home that she would neither visit her neighbors nor make the people who ventured to her tumbling-down place feel welcome.

Those few people who chanced to see her spread the news of a swift change in her appearance, for once she had been a beautiful woman. Now her face was haggard and wrinkled and a frosty fuzz appeared about her lips and chin as moss takes to a decaying tree stump. Her teeth became scattered and snaggled and gave the appearance of old snags rising from a stagnant swamp pool. Her hair, like dead grey moss, fell in tangles almost to her feet. A dingy, yellow and tattered dress scarcely covered her nakedness.

She would not listen to news about her neighbors; and

once she said she knew all about them anyway, for she was certain they were up to their usual gossip and unkind doings.

A strange disease began to kill large numbers of cattle foraging the open range. Yet suspicion was not cast upon the hermit woman, for epedimics among livestock had been known before.

But when people began to die of a malady which none of the wise herb women understood and the corpses were left with the same horrid expression seen on the face of the hermit's dead husband, whispers of fear went almost silently from household to household.

Then one night family and friends stood by a dying woman who in her ravings described threatening and creeping monsters upon the walls and joists. Eventually, as death stole in a warm gust whisked from the sick bed and out the door. Some looked into the moonlight night with glancing pursuit. A creature with satin-black skin and about the size and shape of a cat was seen to jump onto the wattle yard fence, pause a moment and leap into the deep shadows.

Dogs were called out, and they took a group of men along the pathway and footbridge to the hermit's cabin. They found the old woman sitting before the fire, seemingly in a trance and chanting some weird-sounding ditty.

The woman was brought to trial and found guilty of bewitching and inflicting mortal injury upon her neighbors. The sentence was death by fire.

Large crowds, with many people from afar, gathered upon the appointed execution day. They roared with delight as the haggard figure was led to the scene, lashed securely to a post with ropes of rattan vine, and pitch pine splinters were stacked high about her.

The splinter pyre was lit; the flames spit hungrily as they leaped up into growing billows of black smoke.

Then came a shrieking voice—rising somehow above

the shouts of the crowd—from the pyre asking for "one last wish." A justice thought it not unreasonable to, "Let me die with one arm free!" And he slit the bonds of the woman's right arm.

Quickly—he and everyone knew his mistake.

The woman brought from hiding her "witchcraft ball" and tossed it into the air. It streaked like a meteor into the eastern sky unrolling like a ball of yarn while she held to one end of the magic string. She broke her bonds with a surge of superhuman strength. Still—the maddened people swelled about and seized her. To no avail! She tore from their grasp and rose into the air following the string.

As the elated witch soared away eastward she shreiked back mockingly, "I'm going home to London . . . home to London . . . to London . . . London . . ." until the sky swallowed both her and her cries.

The Brandy Witches

Apples grew in abundance in old Carolina, and that meant apple brandy—in Gates County, good apple brandy.

Brandy became a tradition. As late as 1899 Dr. Thomas M. Rdidick, writing in "The Economist" of Elizabeth City, compared it with the county's esteemed race horses and beautiful and captivating girls.

Everybody—all classes—drank brandy in old Gates— from the yeomanry to the gentry. It was as standard as corn pones, and it was as comonplace as the fights at political rallies and horse races and cock fights.

Brandy was in such plenty that brandy houses, like smokehouses and slave-quarters, numbered among the small structures standing about the plantation's Great House. Cider mills ground and pressed away forming rivulets of juice in all communities up to the opening of the twentieth century.

Yet amidst the brandy-plenty there were some people who either had limited supplies or were so thirsty they soon had none.

This was a problem that the Devil took a look into back in the early times when he was so active riding herd over hordes of witches and other indentures.

He came up with the answer—a limited contract, an abundance of brandy throughout the contractual period.

The scheme had a tremendous impact. Those people who had kegged their contemplated needs began to anxiously watch their barrels go dry all too fast. At the same time some of their poor neighbors seemed to have eternal tired and disheveled hangovers. In fact, at times these characters looked almost as wasted as if a witch had been riding them each night for months.

Yet these men were not witches in the strict sense. They were given the power to pass through key holes of brandy houses, but it was not their duty to plague the people of the countryside as nocturnal terrors.

The deal must have been an appealing one, for by the Revolution brandy witches had become so numerous they were an intolerable nuisance. So much that special steps were taken to get rid of them.

A variety of devices were used. Those in the habit of passing through key holes had their skins—which were left outside—sprinkled with salt and pepper. When they emerged from the company of the casks their happiness turned into a nightmare. They could no longer live in their skins and had to wander as lost spirits, die of hunger and thirst or come to some other equally horrid end.

Others were caught trespassing. These were the ones who did not shed their skins but gained entry to the brandy house by some artful device and became invisible while enjoying the elixir of the apple. Unfortunately, intoxication unloosened their tongues and upon utterance of their first word the spell was broken and they resumed their visible form.

The fight against brandy theft mounted to such proportions that soon after the Revolution, the brandy witch had become rare.

Witch-Like Grandma

Witchcraft lore was quite prevalent in most communities as the twentieth century arrived. Adrian Parker, as a boy near Maney's Ferry in the 1890's, was one of many young people who "enjoyed seeing Grandma coming to visit." For Grandma provided a fearful and captivating sort of animation to the lonely countryside. She and the other story tellers "looked the way they imagined the witches did and were the ones who scared you to death." At other times neighbors visited until about ten o'clock at night, and believing children listened to their "old wives tales."

This lore had been rooted in the colonial period when John Lawson observed the English, like the Indian, amused themselves with stories of the never-ending struggle of the spirit realm. Only the Indians told their "many Lying Stories of Spirits and conjurers" to no disadvantage to themselves. Unlike the English, says Lawson, the Indians

"are never fearful of the Night, nor do the Thoughts of Spirits ever trouble them; such as the many Hobgoblins and Bugbears that we suck in with our Milk, and the Foolery of our Nurses and Servants suggests to us; who by their idle Tales of Fairies, and Witches, make such Impressions on our tender years, that at Maturity, we carry Pigmies' Souls in Giants' Bodies and ever after, are thereby so much deprived of Reason, and unmanned, as never to be Masters of half the Bravery Nature designed for us."

[214]

The witch lore, although basically similar to that of the colonial period, was made realistic by adaptation to local people and situations.

St. Johns Wort, gathered on magical June 24, hanged about the homes of the poor to frighten the witches away and to add evidence of the witch threat. To this the good people contributed a large assortment of other tested controls against the haggy terrors.

Witch of Harrell's Ridge

Before the birth of Mrs. Nora Morgan in 1883 the witch of Harrell's Ridge in the Hall area of Gates County became an intolerable annoyance to her neighbors, and they took stern measures to discipline her.

Once she had been a beautiful woman with a hard working husband and a large family, but eventually her husband died and all her children moved away. Time and hardships ruled she should become a lonely hermit "humped and stumpy with long dingy grey hair." Her possessions were reduced to an old clay pipe, a tumbling-down one-room slab house shrouded with wild vines and a few pieces of worn furniture.

Once witch-like—old, ugly and fussy—the woman was suspected of seeking out the company of the Devil and his evil flock. Both people and horses were taken out and ridden at night, and each morning other domestic animals seemed to be wearied out.

Eventually the people became so tired of the witch's mischief her picture was carved into the bark of a beech tree and a witness sent to her home. A gun blast sent a load of silver into the picture, and the witness saw the witch "fall over her wash tub like a dead rabbit."

She survived a long illness but ever afterwards went humped over.

Spiteful Fort Island Witch

Fort Island had a spiteful old witch about the same time—especially after Spencer Eure caught her riding his horse at night and shot her with the silver taken from an umbrella staff.

For some time the pipe-smoking, scrawny old spinster went around the countryside bare-footed and with one arm bandaged up.

Peaceful conditions didn't last. Taking the form of a goose the witch flew screaming in front of Eure's horse, made him run away and dump the Eure family into the roadway. Dry cackles from the nearby swamp told of the witch's delight.

She told John Eure, Spencer's brother, where he could find a doe deer and then led Eure's dog on such a chase that he "ran himself almost to death."

The struggle between the witch and her neighbors went on unceasingly. Women delighted in turning their bonnets wrong side outwards when they saw her coming down the path," and all the known devices to annoy a witch were used.

Eventually the witch died, and neighbors gave her the customary funeral with sobbing and crying and a home-made box for her earthly remains.

The funeral was little different from others—except one small girl wailed to the top of her voice terror-stricken while other people just sobbed, whimpered and sniffled.

Why? Only the child knew until she was grown. It was then she explained the witch had stuttered; the girl, too, had stutered. Before the witch's death she had told the girl, "If you don't stop your stuttering, when I die I'm coming back and scratch your eyes out!"

That explained also why the girl never stuttered after the witch's death.

Wiggins Cross Roads Witch

At Wiggins Cross Roads in lower Gates County the appearance of "gossips in their starch-stiff fly bonnets and pastel aprons" heralded the first days of spring. W. S. Wiggins would remark, "Spring is here. The old witches and buzzards are out from hibernating, and you'll hear a big 'stir-up' in the neighborhood now."

Wiggins, his gossips and witches have since been celebrated at family reunions, says Mrs. O. C. Turner.

Of chief interest was one old gossip who lived deep in the woods at the end of a lonely footpath. She was unfriendly to everyone except a few friends. Eventually she was discovered to be a witch, and as time passed she became an intolerable nuisance to the neighborhood. She took special delight in leading dogs on a circuitous chase as a deer, a fox or other animal and then run home and get in bed.

The hunters grew tired of her mischief, and one frustrated man shot a rabbit-like creature with silver. Instantly it disappeared, and next day friends found the woman suffering from an illness she would not disclose. But a few days later neighbors preparing her body for burial discovered she had died of a gunshot wound containing silver pellets.

The Devil in His Many Forms

CHAPTER XX

Good and Bad Spirits

Although witch stories were generally appreciated by the English and Scotch settlers of old Carolina the Devil and lesses spirits also provided the basis for a considerable amount of lore.

There were good spirits as well as bad, but the good ones were regarded much as guardians and were little talked about.

The new country—with dark woods creeping to the corners of the wattled fences enclosing the small homes—was naturally suited to stories about the mysterious workings of the invisible world. Unexplored depths of great forests, pocosins, swamps and dismals provided sanctuary for the demons by day while they flocked over the entire countryside on dark nights.

An awareness of the invisible world was intensified by the stories imported fresh from the Mother Country and the polytheistic religious concepts among the Indian neighbors and the Negro slaves. By the Revolution a vast amount of lore had been adapted to local situations.

The small farmers, yeomen, poor whites, free Negroes and slaves apparently preferred stories of mystery, intrigue and horror to drive away the reality of toil and hardships.

Place names are suggestive of environmental influence upon the spirit lore. The great swamps or "dismals" harbored both evil spirits and grotesque animals in their dark and gloomy recesses. Dark or black woods and pocosins were associated with the Devil and evil spirits.

Lucifer was credited with plowing out the crooked rivers and creeks of the coastal plains to provoke the sailors. A Devil's Elbow as found in Hertford and Bertie counties was the most difficult of bends for sailing ships to negotiate. A no less provoking obstacle designed by the Devil himself was "No Man's Friend" at the mouth of Bennetts Creek.

No Man's Friend

Because of its deep water, Bennetts Creek was the chief commercial thoroughfare to the central part of Gates County until early in the twentieth century. From colonial times it had been used by sailing craft of many sizes, from the rigged dugout canoe to the three-master schooner.

But at the creek's mouth upon the Chowan River No Man's Friend stood an evil guard like the Devil himself. Here an unfriendly force seemed ever at work devising obstacles and hazards for all navigators.

Sometimes the force was so strong as to make it impossible to sail a ship from the creek into the river—because of a quirk.

The creek enters the river with a huge bow-like curve after running almost parallel to it for several miles. Thus the sailing ship was turned in the opposite direction of its former course. Toiling sailors had to haul in the canvas and pole their craft at the risk or running aground on a mud flat or losing poling depth at the quick drop-off.

Here water expanses spread for miles in three directions—up, down and across the widened river. If a breeze is stirring elsewhere, a stiff and angry wind is blowing here.

The river's wind-controlled tides usually buck the wind

at the creek's mouth; and the combined forces send billowing waves across the shallows . . . to make sailors' lips burn with profanity and to stir a prayer for deliverance in the heart of the small boatman.

Tragedy at Ballard's Racetrack

The Devil frequently appeared in disguise at horse races and cock fights where drinking, gambling and fighting were prominent features of festivities. Apparation and devil-inspired events caused several racetracks over the state to be called Devil's Racetrack.

Although the Devil never gave his name to Ballard's Racetrack in the Hall area of Gates County he was said to have paid it numerous visits.

He was seen time and again as a tall nattily dressed stranger, and he probably would never have been discovered except for his hat—which had a tall stovepipe crown arching forward—and a tragely on the track.

Upon that memorable day this stranger was standing opposite the old mulberry tree in the middle of the track as Mills Eure's fine racing stallion came down the way ahead a length. The stranger detracted the horse's attention, and the horse couldn't seem to take his eyes off of him. Thus the the stallion plunged headlong with the rider into the mulberry tree. Both died of injuries.

In the ensuing melee the stranger's hat was brushed off, and a number of people gasped in shock. The tall hat had covered a long horn which arched forward from the top of the stranger's head. Discovered, the Devil disappeared as quickly as seen.

The fatal race was often rerun by the restless spirits of the horse and rider. Upon many a dark misty night the sound of a horse's hoofs were heard to rise from the eastern end of the track and move westward to the mulberry tree. A light accompanied and vanished with the sound.

DEVIL DISCOVERED AT RACETRACK TRAGEDY

The Devil left other imprints scattered over the countrysides, like the Devil's Woodpile quagmire in Northampton County and dark moody Devil's Gut and Black Gut.

Black Mingle Pocosin

Black Mingle Pocosin was singled out for a great variety of activities. Not only was it frequented by the Devil, it was one of the favorite haunts of his lesser spirits.

This dreadful three-mile-wide wilderness between Hazelton and Wiggins Cross Roads of north central Gates County was surrounded by several plantations which supported large slave populations.

The pocosin also was the habitation of the feared black panther and other treacherous wild creatures which could be heard crying from behind the impenetrable walls of its tightly-woven thickets, and sometimes they showed their frightful forms upon the shadowy borders.

The jack-o'-lantern ventured to the borders almost nightly with his torch to lure people to disaster.

Deep within, beyond prying human eyes, evil spirits frolicked in grotesque human and animal forms.

No person ever built a house in Black Mingle Pocosin, but there was a pathway as old as tradition which cut through its eastern side near Wiggins Cross Roads.

This narrow way, encroached upon by pine and gum trees and gallberry thickets, was so feared that some people would not travel it alone. And with good cause—the Devil had been seen in its shadows, sometimes as a large dog and at others as a black beast—with eyes glowing like fire coals and belching forth red smoke from his mouth and nostrils.

Other spirits made their appearance much like those in a tale by Isabella Kinght, a slave woman on John Knight's plantation.

"Aunt Fereby, She Won't Drink It!"

Long before Isabella was born on the John Knight plantation, a very old woman had visited too late one afternoon on the opposite side of Black Mingle Pocosin; for the sun was setting as she reached the pocosin path.

The way grew very dark, so dark she had to tap out the running of the footbridges with her walking cane. As the darkness deepened a loud rumbling noise arose from deep within the pocosin. The wind blew up a black boiling thunderstorm. The old woman hurried to the side of the pocosin to an "off-cast" house.

This house had been abandoned so long that it was falling to pieces and passage could be gained only by beating back the thorn bushes and creeping vines.

The storm struck with fury. Trees were uprooted and rain fell in torrents while the house creaked and groaned above the noise of the storm.

Then within there were whispering noises which told that drinks were being passed around. But no one could be seen as lightning flashes turned things a pale grey. Strangeness of the sounds suggested that these were witches' potions.

Suddenly a voice cried aloud, "Aunt Fereby, she won't drink it!"

"If she won't drink it, I'll make her drink it!" came a stern reply.

Badly frightened, the old woman ran from the house. Quickly her fears were justified. The storm vanished, and in its place light from the set sun spread across a cloudless sky.

Varied Devil Forms

During the colonial period the Devil assumed a large variety of forms, but after the Revolution lore became more uniform and he appeared in a limited number of disguises.

Dreams, visions and apparitions contributed to the early physical representations. Across the countrysides, from the pocosin recesses to the pine barrens and plantations, Old Lucifer was seen variously as a black ball, a red ball of fire, a wicked animal, or a fraudulent man. He took the form of a goat, a cow or some other domestic animal. However, his most dreadful apparition was as a black bear or panther with fiery red eyes and mouth. As a man he commonly was a jolly and scheming white fellow or a black fiend with fiery eyes and mouth. Sometimes he had a horn on his head which was hidden by a curling lock of hair and a long forked tail, and as a stranger he always bore an odd mark recognizable by people of sharp wit.

Evangelists of the early nineteenth century seem to have had a great influence on ante-bellum Devil forms. This is suggested by a published account of the Rev. William Glendinning's encounters with Satan. Glendinning was a close friend of Bishop Asbury, who traveled as a missionary after the Revolution.

The Devil first appeared with a face as "black as any coal—his eyes and mouth as red as blood." He gnashed together "long white teeth."

At another time the Devil "appeared upward to five feet high," and about the top of his head "there seemed a bulk, like a body, but bigger than any person; about 15 or 18 inches from the ground there appeared something like legs, and under them, feet; but no arms or thighs . . . When he moved, it was as an armful of chains rattling together."

A third time the Devil was "like a four-footed beast, as large as a calf of a year old, and seemed to have large wings." He was driven away by loudly mentioning the name of the Lord to him, at which he would "stand trembling, while the balls of fire would be flaming out of his eyes." Unable to stand long he would draw back and disappear "as quick as lightning."

Restless Evil Spirits

Hordes of restless spirits, ever active on eerie missions, added to the uneasy state of the countrysides. Ghosts seemed everywhere. They flocked into the pine barrens where they took the appearance of the grey box face pine, and in later years they stood amidst the grey granite markings of cemeteries. Their chief delight was to make their presence be felt without being seen, except as a fleeting apparition to freeze the heart stone-cold.

Creatures of the low grounds, swamps and branches lent their shapes to mischievious spirits to be seen shadow-like about the forest recesses or to pass across a darkened path. A balking or shying horse told of the presence of a spirit his master could not see.

Evil spirits were heard. Along the trails through the dark forests the trees—especially the slender tall pine—creaked and moaned as manifestation of lonely spirit dwellers.

Some spirits let their presence be known by indirect devices. Common signs of their presence were a warm current of air or a grey vapor at night.

By various manifestations, spirits of the dead and the possessed living seemed to greatly outnumber the good people of the countrysides.

Fairies and Swamp Demons

CHAPTER XXI

Survival of the Fairies

European immigrants—especially indentured servants—were charged no extra passage for the many fairies and other spirits they brought with them to the American colonies.

However, the good fairies did not thrive too well upon the American frontiers even though fairy tales were extremely popular in Mother England and other European countries about 1700 to 1850.

It wasn't so much that the delicate sprites were not liked as it was the Devil, witches, ghosts and other frightful things provided too much competition.

Nonetheless, between and about the Chowan River and Dismal swamps lore provides evidence that throughout the ante-bellum period little people danced in the meadows, played pranks on people, brought children from the underground, stole them away, spun fantastic bowers, and had a finger in many other things mysterious.

Babies were brought to the plantations of Old Gates by the little people. Isabella Knight, a slave woman on the John Knight plantation at Wiggins Cross Roads who survived the Civil War almost a half-century, stated they came from the underground through stump holes which were the surface outlets to the subterranean tunnels.

Stories were woven about evil fairies which found sanctuary in Dismal Swamp where they kept company of jack-o'-lanterns, witches, and grotesque creatures.

A vague sort of fairy lore seemed commonplace. This included the notion that subterranean spirits and little people came to the earth's surface by little tunnels in the deep woods, grassy savannahs and reed-choked pocosins. The openings of the tunnels were artfully covered by wisps of straw or tufts of grass made to look like rabbit beds or fox dens. The small people of the swamps were constantly at work interlacing grass into small cradles.

The lore seems to have been as varied as each individual's imagination with the fairies doing everything from weaving stirrups like those made by witches in the horse's mane to decorating the swamp trees with streaming grey moss.

The little people worked tirelessly guiding the hand of Nature to create scenes of indescribable beauty. A contributor to "The North Carolinian" in 1872 mirrows this technique. While sailing down the narrow Dismal Swamp bordered Pasquotank River, "Old grape vines and bitter sweet stretch up from the river's edge and side banks for many feet. . . . Away up in mid-air fairy bowers are formed, where nymphs of wood and water meet."

Vague faceless powers—especially noticeable in the Hall area of Gates County—were harmless enough when left alone but became terrors when disturbed. They were thought to dwell in the far-away and lonely places except when awakened and summoned, and their chief habitat was the mysterious swamps.

The Cold Supper

"Don't you try it! Better not disturb the spirits!" old wives invariably warned the young woman when she began talking of setting a cold supper at midnight to learn the identity of her future husband.

Tradition was against the hazard. Upon many occasions

the spirits awakened from their slumber had gotten out of hand and brought disaster.

However, a courageous young woman, upon the approach of midnight, could activate the foretelling powers by setting two plates with nine different foods on each. If as the clock chimed the hour of twelve a man came in and seated himself at the table, he would be the future husband; but if a coffin floated in, the woman would remain a stale maid.

One poor girl had fainted and died at the sight of the coffin, it was told, when she could have broken the spell by running from the room.

Another time neither a man nor a coffin came. Instead, a cyclone arose from the swamp, cut a swath through the forest, and ripped off one end of the house with the chimney before the woman fled terror-stricken.

The intended husband also was put to danger. He had to cross over water, and one man was drowned in the river while enroute to his girl's home.

Yet the mother and grandmother cited thrilling stories of having previewed their martial bliss. They knew that the man who cut into his food deeply with his knife would make a mean husband and the one who cut into it lightly and carefully would be a good and kind one.

The Treasure Guardians

People both to the east and west of the Chowan River told numerous stories of Blackbeard the pirate and his hidden treasures — especially the large chest upon the river flats below Holidays Island and the one he and his men were seen pushing overboard at the mouth of Spikes Creek.

Nonetheless, nearby Scratch Hall paid little attention to Blackbeard. The area had its own private treasure trove, somewhere on "Money Island," a swamp island which old timers also knew as Crawford Island.

This uninhabited narrow sand ridge was less than a mile long and barely more than a mile from the nearest home. But to those children listening to Old Granny of the pitch-pine torch and the kerosene lamp eras it was a mysterious far-away place. It was surrounded by the fearful bogs of the Chowan River swamp, shrouded by the mystery of its own forest, and guarded by big snakes, hungry bears and panthers while its fabulous treasure was watched over by the wicked swamp spirits.

Even wise Old Granny was uncertain how the treasure came to be buried in the island's sands; but older children going there with grownups tea-berry picking could see an "off-cast" log cabin tumbling and decaying beneath a mat of vines. Perhaps some hermit hunter or a settler of long forgotten years had deposited his treasure not far from his unmarked grave, the children were told.

Holes in the earth were evidence of as many unsuccessful attempts to recover the treasure. One midwife identified the larger of the holes as the "Money Hole" where the treasure had been discovered but not retrieved because of intervention by the swamp spirits.

Traditional stories provided stern warning that he who went seeking the treasure chanced the vengeance of its guardian spirits. Once creatures like boar hogs had come from the woods and cut up two men with their long tusks. One fellow went onto the island alone, found a pot of money, but had his hand cut off with a phantom sword as he sought to lift it from the earth. Two men were driven away by a buzzing noise which grew unbearably intense as they sank their hole deeper.

Aware of previous failures, two new adventurers took all known precautions against awakening the swamp spirits. One bright moonlight night they crept silently through the forests and across the bogs to their chosen digging site on Money Island. They spaded silently and carefully beside the eerie homestead ruins during the magic minutes before midnight. Soon one digger cried aloud, "I've found it!"

The uneasy guardian spirits were awakened, and their anger arose as a whirring sound deep within the surrounding swamp. The noise grew into a cyclone which ripped through the swamp forest and spun a cloud of debris across the face of the moon. Inky darkness fell over the island and streaks of light flashed about forming the forms of demons. Thunder snapped and rolled like the snarls and growls of fighting wild beasts.

The treasure seekers fled for their lives and never ventured again to Money Island.

Varied Spirit Controls

The spirit controls—many common to other areas—seemed endless. They became so interwoven with the forest dwellers' language that a simple allusion often conveyed subtle traditional wisdom. Some controls had special local significance.

For example, upon a winter night when a neighbor's dogs were heard to tree in the nearby swamp, an old man or old woman might be heard to spitefully say, "I'm going to cut his dog off." Whereupon, a chunk of wood lying amidst the fireplace embers would be upended with its smoking end pointing up the chimney. As the smoke hissed from the charred wood the spell-caster might say, "He won't be hearing from his dog any more tonight."

Upon the nearby plantation a rock was kept in the fire at all times to hinder the hawk. So long as the rock was hot the hawk might strike a chicken but a mystic power would draw him aside for a miss.

PART 6

Civil War Anarchy

CHAPTER XXII

Bread Baskets for Two Armies

Gates County—like other counties along the Chowan River—was invaded by no major military force during the Civil War. She, instead, was permitted to become a part of a no-man's-land and to serve as a bread basket for both Union and Confederate armies, an avenue for contraband trade and a sanctuary for deserters and conscription evaders who turned murderers and thieves.

Isolated with her problems and abused by all, Gates suffered longer and more than her neighbors. As the war years advanced divisions among her people so weakened civil authority that she had a little civil war of her own, with desperate outlaws moving under the cover of the forests and of the night.

Neighbor slew neighbor during the struggle, and inflamed passions brought on vengeance killings afterwards.

The tide of violence began near the end of the first year of the war as the Yankees secured the Norfolk, Virginia, area, entrenched themselves on the North Carolina coast and their gunboats took charge of the Albemarle Sound and moved at will upon the Chowan River.

The Chowan River became the mythical line of demarkation between Yankee and Rebel territory, with the counties to the west within Confederate lines and those to the east, Union lines.

Thus Gates technically was in Union territory, but both Confederate and Yankee foraging and raiding parties moved through her countrysides taking up what they pleased with practically no resistance.

By fall 1861 the deteriorating influence of war began to appear. In November the "Daily Express" of Petersburg, Virginia, said that "some vile incendiaries have been lurking about Sunbury" and that a number of houses had been burned. A few days before George Costen, a wealthy planter, had lost a barn, stables and carriage house with 1,000 bushels of corn, 100 bushels of wheat and a large quantity of fodder and other articles.

Midway the war the Confederates opened commissaries to the west of the Chowan River and funneled out supplies from Gates—and other counties to the east—to supply Lee's Army of Virginia. Their purchasing agents moved freely throughout the area bringing in cotton wanted by the Yankees and bringing out bacon, other foods and supplies.

In June 1863 General James Longstreet sent Benning with a foraging party into the counties east of the Chowan, and in February 1864 General George Pickett led a similar group into the area.

July 1863 Colonel J. B. Spear's cavalry passed through from Norfolk to Winton on a raid intended for the railroad bridge at Weldon. However, he was stopped a few miles short at Boon's Mill in Northampton County.

As the war progressed contraband grew in demand by both sides. By 1864 New England textile mills were hit by cotton shortage, and Major General Benjamin F. Butler with jurisdiction over the northeastern counties permitted and encouraged trade with the Confederates.

Treasury regulations allowed farmers to come into Union lines to buy "family supplies." Their wagons moved without hindrance through thinly manned Union picket lines, and supplies then moved across the no-man's-land

COL. SPEAR'S CAVALRY PASSING THROUGH THE SWAMP.

COL. SPEAR PASSES THROUGH CHOWAN RIVER SWAMP

into Confederate territory. The "farmers" bought cotton from the Confederates and sold it to northern merchants for salt, sugar and other merchandise. They used salt to preserve their pork which was sold to the Confederates for more cotton.

The most used water route for contraband was from Norfolk through the Dismal Swamp Canal to the Albemarle Sound, and up the Chowan River and its tributaries to Confederate depots. An extensive overland trade was conducted from Elizabeth City through Perquimans and Gates counties to the Chowan River at Winton and on to the Confederate depots. A lesser flow of contraband moved across the Dismal Swamp along the Hamburg Ditch to Holley Grove in Gates and then overland to its destination.

Destructive "Buffaloes"

A group of deserters and conscription evaders known as "Buffaloes" became a destructive force in the second year of the war, and before conclusion of the conflict their activity contributed largely to creation of a state of anarchy.

The first group of these men were the North Carolina Union Volunteers, but later the term also applied to deserters from both armies who pillaged, stole, burned and murdered as they gathered up commodities for their own subsistence and the contraband trade.

The "Buffs" came mostly from the non-slaveholding classes who soon after the outbreak of the war found themselves without a cause. Many of them had responded to the first calls for enlistment, but when they had a real taste of war and became obsessed with the notion this was "a rich man's war and a poor man's fight" they declined to reenlist and avoided conscription. Spread of Yankee influence over this area apparently was an encouraging factor to evasion.

Notorious Jack Fairless

John A. (Jack) Fairless of Gates County's Mintonsville Township between the Old Town and Indian Neck
roads, became one of the more notorious. buffaloes, as
commander of Company E of the First North Carolina
Union Volunteers.

The son of a small farmer, Fairless had acquired a lawless reputation by age of 21. He was arrested near Suffolk,
Virginia, in 1861, for theft of a mule and cart, says Thomas
C. Parramore in "The Roanoke-Chowan Story." A few
days after enlisting on February 28, 1862, with Captain
Julian Gilliam's Company C of the 52nd North Carolina
Regiment at Gatesville he was accused of theft from a
fellow soldier. For this offense Fairless had one side of his
head shaved, then was put into an inverted barrel and
driven around Gatesville with his fellow soldiers beating
on it with sticks. Fairless reacted by promptly deserting
and going over to the Union at Roanoke Island.

After serving a short time as a pilot for various Union
operations along the coast, Fairless was given permission
by Col. Rush Hawkins to raise recruits for a Buffalo company.

Fairless headed homeward, and August 6, after recruit-
ing in upper Chowan and lower Gates counties, he wrote
Gen. John G. Foster he had "succeeded in raising men for
my company beyond expectation, having now seventy five
with the prospect of a hundred in a few days." Already
with looting in mind, Fairless suggested that with permission "I could collect a sufficient number of horses to
mount them from this region, and also plenty of forage."

After the next day's enlistment Fairless actually had
only about forty men, composed chiefly of deserters and
conscription evaders. By August 13 the group had established themselves on Wingfield farm, traditional Chowan
County home of the Brownrigg family, then owned by Dr.
Richard Dillard, absent in Virginia. The farm was easy to

defend from land and its frontage on the Chowan River provided communication with and protection by Union gun boats.

Fairless said he had raised the company "for the purpose of protecting the Union citizens in. Gates, Chowan and Perquimmons counties," but Parramore says his foraging expeditions "deteriorated into raids of plunder and destruction."

An Edenton citizen wrote to the Raleigh "Register" October 12, 1862, that ". . . it would be difficult indeed to record the evils which these ruffians have inflicted upon the people of that neighborhood and surrounding country. . . . They have allured off hundreds of our Negroes and continue to steal them."

Fairless didn't hesitate to rob his old neighbors. But when he came to the home of Mrs. Mary Wiggins the lady blocked the stairway and said sternly, "Jack, you know I keep my provisions upstairs, but if you go up, it will be over my dead body!" Fairless ordered his men from the house and soon followed them. Fairless also went away without the family's nice colt. A son, W. S. Wiggins, too young for military service, had hidden it in a swamp.

When Dick Rountree came home on furlough he rejected an invitation to desert and sign up with Fairless company. Afterwards Fairless heard that Dick had called him a ruffian and the buffaloe swore he would kill him, as he very nearly did. Rountree was confronted on a roadway, but he fled into the woods with Fairless' men firing at him. Later he was trapped at home but he hid up the chimney. He withstood the smoke from a small fire as Fairless and his men, swearing they planned to "unjoint him joint by joint," searched the house in vain.

When on September 19 Lt. Commander Charles Flusser, chief of the Union naval forces in the Albemarle region, dispatched Lt. Thomas J. Woodard to investigate rumors about "our home guard thieves at Wingfield," only twenty of the sixty-three recruits were found in camp and Captain Fairless was "in a state of intoxication" threatening to shoot some of his men. It was found that "all the ammunition has been smuggled out and sold to citizens for liquor."

Fairless was temporarily unseated, but a trip to Roanoke Island rewarded him with "clothing and ammunition, sugar and coffee" from Col. Howard who reaffirmed his confidence in him. Fairless also got a tough drill master, George Alden, for the 100 men he contemplated enlisting.

October 25, after a brief absence from camp, Alden reported Fairless had gone out "on a reconnaissance with 8 men on Wednesday last, he being intoxicated, and got into a dispute with one of the privates named Jim Wallace (a Gates County private who had deserted Company C, 19th N. C. Regiment) and shot at him but missed fire, he being so drunk, and before he could fire again the said private shot him dead."

The company got a new commander and better discipline, but the Confederates had determined to rid the country of the Buffalo nuisance. After two Confederate attacks on the fort and receipt of intelligence that Gen. James Longstreet was sending a large supply train into Gates and Chowan Counties accompanied by five hundred cavalrymen, April 16, 1863, the Buffaloes abandoned Wingfield and never returned.

Countrysides Stripped of Provisions

"The citizens of Gates County are now rid of the despicable foe," wrote a lieutenant of Company C, 63rd Regiment North Carolina Troops in the "Daily Progress" of Raleigh two weeks after the evacuation of Wingfield.

He touched on a sensitive subject by observing the conscript law had not been enforced in the county and saying "I wish some one would come through here and raise a battalion of strong young men. I think, judging from their shy looks, that they would make good rangers. They would certainly easily learn to 'sege,' though there might be some difficulty in rallying them."

Longstreet's expedition had been a success "as everything has been taken out safely" and "immense quantities of provisions have been saved by us in Gates and adjoining counties."

Although the Yankees did not open another Buffalo camp east of the Chowan River, as the Partisan Rangers feared they might, underground Buffalo activity developed in all the counties of the northeastern area and particularly in Gates. Here civil authority was undermined by increasing numbers of deserters, conscription evaders, and opportunists who infested the deep woods and swamps and came out in bands by night to rob, pillage and murder.

The Partisan Rangers protested loudly when their companies were ordered to report out of the enemy lines for regular service. Longstreet's presence at Suffolk would not curb the lawlessness, it was asserted. Moreover, the Ranger companies had been formed from volunteers beyond the conscript age, men with honorable discharges, and boys not old enough for the army "to fight as much as they could for their families." Removal of these home guardsmen would permit "the Yankees and negroes steal and plunder and insult and outrage their families and leave the country utterly desolate." Longstreet actually had "left us ten times worse off than before."

The Buffaloes—some with families and sons or brothers fighting with the Confederacy—"were generally the lowest characters in the community—the most ignorant, though possessing to a degree that low cunning instinctive in the animal race. Some men and women "occupying positions in society of responsibility" were leagued with them. These people "became so insufferable" that the "citizens armed themselves and by watching their opportunities succeeded in taking prisoners and killing a good number." causing their raids to be less frequent.

The swamps east of the Chowan River, intersected by numerous sand ridges and dotted with small islands, provided the chief hideouts for desperate bands of lawless men who had turned Buffalo. The Scratch Hall area became notorious for their activity, as explained in the September 9, 1871, "Southern Magazine" of Baltimore: "As civil courts had been suspended for three or four years in that section, the people drifted into a state of anarchy. Good men had no redress at law, consequently they soon became the prey of desperate characters, and murders and robberies were the order of the day. . . ."

Few families were spared the raiding Buffalo gangs. Women and children, especially the poor, were made to suffer great privation.

The experience of many housewives was similar to that of Mrs. Martha Umphlett. While her husband was at the battle front she lived alone with their children in a one-room log house on the Scratch Hall pine barrens. One day a group of armed men came and took all her meat and sparse supplies and drove away the horse and cow. The horse was needed to till a few acres of corn, sweet potatoes and sugar cane. Loss of the cow, which foraged the lowlands and pocosins for her own keep, reduced the small children to near starvation.

Several men bought spoils from small Buffalo groups and traded with the Yankes. One Hinton at Roberts Landing on Bennetts Creek became notorious for his large business in contraband. Yankee boats could come up the creek from the Chowan River to his landing without fear of Confederate attack. Wide miry swamps made it impossible for either cavalry or artillery to come within range of the stream.

Loot, which consisted chiefly of salt meat, provisions

and livestock, was usually moved to him by night. Out of this trade comes a story as related by Andrew Cross:

One night when two Buffaloes were driving stolen cattle to Hinton one of the herd grew tied and laid down about one-half mile from the landing. One man told his companion to go on and make delivery.

Returning a short while later the companion discovered the first man had slain the cow with a fence rail and had steaks prepared for a feast.

Brands no longer protected cattle on the open range. Herds were destroyed as Buffaloes hunted down these animals with dogs and killed them.

Bob Dukes was one of the first Buffaloes killed in the Scratch Hall section. Several people charged him with theft, and when stolen goods were found in his possession the Partisan Rangers stood him before a firing squad of twelve men near present Eure's Christian Church. Among these men were several of Dukes' neighbors, and to ease their conscience one of the guns was rammed with powder and wadding only.

Serious Deterioration by End of 1863

By December 1863 conditions of the country east of the Chowan River had suffered serious deterioration. A corespondent of "The Petersburg Express," back from an expedition for pork into Nansemond, Gates and Perquimans counties, had found:

"The negroes have almost all left, and the wagons and teams been taken off. A few broken down horses, mules and carts, only are left on the largest farms. You cannot hire a white man to drive hogs, for ten dollars a day. They are afraid of being informed against, and taken off to Norfolk.

"The citizens seem loyal, but are generally alarmed, expecting every day to be visited by the Yankees. No one who has not visited this beautiful country, can form a correct idea of the miserable condition of the people. They are, exposed daily to the foe, with no hope of relief. The wealthiest inhabitants have been reduced to a state of dependence, and this is a general thing, almost without exception. While pork is the principal thing they have, it seems it has been left only to be fatted and cured for the use of the Federals. Their recent raid near South Mills, has spread terror through that section of the country, the inhabitants having been ordered not to dispose of anything to the Confederates, on pain of having their houses burned, their lands confiscated and themselves sent into our lines.

"Corn is scarce and sells for fifty dollars a barrel.

"The greatest attention is paid to hogs. They are fatted principally on peas and potatoes. . . ."

A letter from near Sunbury March 7, 1864, by an unknown writer, in Blanche Baker's papers, complained:

"One week we have Yankees—the next 'Soldiers,' as the Confederates are called—raided on by all, protected by none. Between the two we shall be used up, if the present state of things exists much longer.

Starvation is very near and at the door of many, always—not far from ours. But amid all our trials, I assure you, Major, speaking of the county of Gates, there is not a more loyal people in the Confeder--acy—notwithstanding what may be said of us, across the River, to the contrary. . . . Provisions are very scarce and high. We have to buy corn; our army is here in considerable force; the very little they leave will not be reached by 'Confederate' (currency) now quite uncurrent. The little I have is in Confederate money. How I shall get through this year, the Lord only knows. . . . We are cut off and live in ignorance of what is going on on either side."

Contraband Business Active

Meanwhile, the contraband business behind the Yankee lines was quite active as indicated by a "Reconniassance of the Chowan" by Lt. Ward, aid-de-camp on General Palmer's staff and reported in the August 2, 1864, "North Carolina Times" of New Bern.

At Winton a large quantity of Confederate salt, bacon and other stores were destroyed and taken were two bales of cotton, two barrels of northern packed pork, and a large quantity of tobacco. Intelligence led an overland force from Gates Ferry to Gatesville to capture the little steamer "Arrow," recently raised at Franklin, Virginia, where she had been sunk early in the war. She had delivered two bales of cotton and two barrels of lard "to await transportation to Elizabeth City and Coinjock, there to sell or exchange on Confederate account with unprincipled traders, who have been evading wholesome military and trade regulations." At Colerain, another smuggling point, about 90 bales of cotton and 100 boxes of tobacco, were seized.

Lt. Ward observed, "It seems that a regular system of blockade running has been carried on under specious pleas, for some months, at Elizabeth City, South Mills, Coinjock, Edenton, and other places, where goods have been freely exchanged for Confederate staples, such as cotton and tobacco, in the hands of Confederate agents. . . ."

Rise of Organized Outlaw Gangs

Confederate officials were informed of oganized Buffalo activity east of the Chowan River by the middle of 1864, but the wildness of the country and a shortage of fighting men prevented action from being taken against them. One Buffalo camp was set up at the Dowry on the Chowan River where plunder was brought and sold to the Yankees and unscrupulous traders. Tradition has listed G. G. Saunders and Mary Eure among the local residents slain by the outlaws.

About six months later, in January 1865, ranks of the Buffaloes had been swelled by deserters from both the Union and Confederate armies, and armed bands of raiders began to scourge the previously unmolested agricultural country to the west of the Chowan River in Hertford County.

C. F. Turner, a Confederate purchasing agent of Camden County, stumbled upon their camp at the log cabin home of mulatto John Lang in a heavily forested area on Potecasi Creek east of Murfreesboro and Winton road.

The Buffaloes "had united and formed a company, and had elected a tall, light-haired man by the name of Williams as their captain, who had left the Federal army, and hailed from the State of New York."

One week earlier a band of these men led by one Johnson, Williams' lieutenant, "had gone to the house of a Mr. Spivey, who was serving at that time in the Confederate army, and demanded of his wife such things as they wished in the way of provisions, clothing, and bed-covering. After having taken from this lady everything they saw that could be made of any use to them, they put some insulting question to her; and having received a spirited answer" Johnson shot her in the head with a shotgun.

As Turner walked uneasily toward the cabin he was "answered only by savage looks mingled with expressions of surprise." But Captain Williams came up and conducted him into the cabin where he saw on a table "old pistols, swords, carbines, bayonets, double - barrelled shot - guns, and rifles," and nearby "some half - dozen or more men in Federal blue overcoats."

The visitor was permitted to go on his way with directions after being relieved—at a price set by the Buffalo captain—of his pistol and knife.

Turner reported to Captain J. B. Heard, an assistant commisary and in command of Confederate forces in the area. The presence of the outlaws were known, Heard replied, but an attack on them had been impossible, bebause they numbered "twice as many men as our entire picket force." Moreover, General Lee was in such need of provisions that all available men were required to guard the commisary supplies.

However, after a series of robberies by the Buffaloes, the citizens sought aid both from Confederate General Lee and Union General Butler. Turner said, "It was reported that Lee and Butler agreed to send men to that section of North Carolina, and that these soldiers should meet in this neutral territory and put down those desperate outlaws . . ." However, a body of Confederate cavalry "crossed the Chowan at South Quays and entered Scratch Hall District, and in less than ten days they had killed as many as twenty-two of these robbers . . ." while the balance left the area. Within a few weeks the war was over.

The Buffaloes were slain without trial. Mrs. Nora Morgan says soldiers came for her grandfather John Horton while he was sitting at the dinner table at his home on Winton Causeway near Story's. Although he protested he had no connection with the Buffaloes he was taken into a nearby bottom and shot. The soldiers hurried on their way in quest of other men.

Johnson had been killed before arrival of the cavalry. He and Captain Williams quarreled over spoils, and Johnson left with a band of followers to set up a camp in Dismal Swamp near South Mills. They stopped at a small cabin near Sandy cross for the night and came out to investigate passerbys. They encountered soldiers and Johnson was shot in an affray.

Violence Lives After War

Spilling the blood of the Buffaloes did not bring a complete end to violence. Hatreds seethed and some old accounts were to be settled, as was the case with illiterate Titus J. "Ty" Lee of Scratch Hall.

The small pine barrens farmer was slain by his neighbors February 3, 1866, ten months after the war.

Lee had been a Buffalo suspect, as a killer of cattle on the open range which made him remembered as "a thief of the first order."

Lee had flown into a rage of anger when John Cross accused him openly. One of Cross' trusted Negroes had come upon Lee at night and discovered a beef in his cart. Lee was quoted as saying, "Look at it well! Now, if you tell, I'll kill you!"

A few days later Cross was shot from an ambush of gallberry bushes as he walked a wooded path. He was painfully injured, but his life was saved because of the weak thrust of the black powder and his dog which drove the assailant, thought to be Lee, away.

Then a tar kiln Cross had prepared near his home was set afire, but cautious Cross sent his slave running to put it out. Lee stepped from hiding and asked, "Where's John?"

His master had sent him to investigate, Lee was told.

"Good thing he didn't come, Lee was quoted as saying; 'I came here to kill him."

Other hostile acts followed. Lee was shot at in the woods, and one neighbor caught him in the field plowing and shot out an eye. Lee threatened, and August 24, 1864, he made a will which acknowledged "the uncertainty of life and the certainty of death" and named his wife Mary A. Lee, and after her, Mills H. Eure beneficiaries.

But tempers of the neighborhood subsided for more than a year, until Lee made renewed threats. His neighbors determined to be rid of him. They called on his home several nights to find he had fled.

The final night a voice came from the darkness, "No need trying your apple tree. We know you have been climbing into it from your upstairs window."

Lee's wife was conducted to a neighbor's house. A door to Lee's house was kicked open. A shotgun blasted into a shadowy form in front of the door. Another flash mortally wounded Lee, who had been tricked into shooting at an overcoat held as a decoy.

Rountree Gets His Revenge

Dick Rountree of Indian Neck, who had been molested by Jack Fairless and his Wingfield Buffaloes in 1862, got his revenge four years after the war—upon Jack's father.

Rountree, on leave from his regiment when the war ended, still had his army rifle. Parramore quotes Hallet Ward as saying, "Dick melted a hand full of squirrel shot into a ball to fit his rifle. Joe Fairless (father of Jack) went to mill every Friday . . . Dick hid himself beside the road in Chapel Swamp where he knew Joe would pass going to the mill—the Old Wiggins Mill near Mintonsville. Dick made a crack shot that hit Joe in the right temple. That was the end of Old Joe. Dick made no secret of it all. . . . He was a member of the Warwick Baptist Church. . . . The Conference took the matter up and by a unanimous vote acquitted Dick with a renewed membership of affection."

Acknowledgements

To those people who contributed traditional material, research assistance and advice in compiling and presenting historical sketches and tales for this work we extend our appreciation.

Dr. Thomas C. Parramore, professor of history, Meredith College; William S. Powell, librarian, North Carolina Collection, University of North Carolina; and E. Frank Stephenson Jr., graduate student, were especially -helpful in library research.

Countless people contributed to the traditional material. Among them are J. D. Baines, Shirley C. Baines, D. E. Barnes, Horace Barnes, Louis Benton, Edward Beverly, J. A. Bowen, Bruce Brady, Mrs. H. B. Castellow, Miss Lucy Costen, John Crawford, Andrew Cross, Wallace Daniels, Mrs. Mary Ellen Crawford Dilday, Mrs. Linda Edwards, Henry Eure, Tazewell Eure, Noah Felton, Henry Flood, Raleigh Futrell, Ben Godwin, Troy Green, Peter Griffith, A. P. Harrell, Mrs. Rosa Jane Eure Harrell, Collie Hawks, Rufus Hewitt, Mrs. Linda Jordan Hofler, Mrs. Della Harrell Israel, C. W. Jones, Tom Jordan, Edward Knight, Mrs. Nora Morgan, Alphin Murray, Oscar Lane, Thurmond Lassiter, Charlie Lawrence, C. E. Mullen, Adrian L. Parker, Frunie Pierce, Clinton Piland, Henry Powell, Hugh Rice, Mrs. Florence Sears, J. W. Sexton, Lannie Smith, Mrs. Lee Smith, Peter Story, Grady Sumner, Mrs. O. C. Turner, W. T. Umphlett, Hersey Ezelle Underwood, Robert Major Vaughan, Butler Williams, H. B. Winslow, Tom Yeates, Mrs. Belle Parker, Mrs. C. H. Carter, Woodrow Felton, and Hallett Ward.

Current histories of North Carolina and Virginia were utilized in conjunction with basic sources, like "Explorations, Description and Attempted Settlement of Carolina 1584-1590," "The North Carolina Colonial Records," "Lawson's History of North Carolina," "William Byrd's Dividing Line Histories," contemporary newspapers, magazines, diaries, travel accounts, and county and state records. Primary sources are mentioned in the text.

Libraries, institutions and agencies which were of vital assistance are:

University of North Carolina Library, Chapel Hill;

D. H. Hill Libarary, N. C. State University, Raleigh;

North Carolina State Library, Raleigh;

North Carolina Deparment of Archives and History, Raleigh;

Duke University Library, Durham, N. C.

University of Virginia Library, Charlottesville;

Virginia State Library, Richmond;

Morgan Memorial Library, Suffolk, Va.;

Norfolk Public Library, Norfolk, Va.;

N. C. Dept. Conservation and Development, Raleigh;

Virginia Chamber of Commerce, Richmond.

[248]

Bacall